AF412274

APQ LIBRARY OF
PHILOSOPHY

APQ LIBRARY OF PHILOSOPHY
Nicholas Rescher, Editor

THE PHILOSOPHY OF CHARLES S. PEIRCE
A Critical Introduction
ROBERT ALMEDER

TWO CENTURIES OF PHILOSOPHY
American Philosophy Since the Revolution
PETER CAWS (ed.)

RATIONAL BELIEF SYSTEMS
BRIAN ELLIS

THE NATURE OF PHILOSOPHY
JOHN KEKES

INTRODUCTION TO THE
PHILOSOPHY OF MATHEMATICS
HUGH LEHMAN

VALUE AND EXISTENCE
JOHN LESLIE

RECENT WORK IN PHILOSOPHY
KENNETH G. LUCEY AND TIBOR R. MACHAN (eds.)

PLATO ON BEAUTY, WISDOM,
AND THE ARTS
JULIUS MORAVCSIK AND PHILIP TEMKO (eds.)

LEIBNIZ
An Introduction to His Philosophy
NICHOLAS RESCHER

THE LOGIC OF INCONSISTENCY
A Study in Nonstandard Possible-World
Semantics and Ontology
NICHOLAS RESCHER AND ROBERT BRANDOM

THE NATURE OF KNOWLEDGE
ALAN R. WHITE

KNOWLEDGE AND SCEPTICISM

DOUGLAS ODEGARD

ROWMAN AND LITTLEFIELD
Totowa, New Jersey

To
Sandra, Eric, and Diane

First published in the United States 1982 by Rowman and Littlefield,
81 Adams Drive, Totowa, New Jersey 07512.

Distributed in the U.K. and Commonwealth by
George Prior Associated Publishers Limited
High Holborn House
53154 High Holborn
London WC1 V 6RL
England

Library of Congress Cataloging in Publication Data
Odegard, Douglas, 1935–
   Knowledge and scepticism.

   (APQ library of philosophy)
   Bibliography: p.
   Includes indexes.
   1. Knowledge, Theory of.   2. Skepticism.
I. Title.   II. Series.
BD161.033   1982   121   81-23478
ISBN 0-8476-7032-5   AACR2

Printed in the United States of America

Contents

INTRODUCTION   1

Part I   The Concept of Knowledge

Chapter 1 PLAUSIBILITY   5
Chapter 2 PROBABILITY   18
Chapter 3 CERTAINTY   31
Chapter 4 TRUTH   40
Chapter 5 KNOWLEDGE   56

Part II   The Justification of Knowledge Claims

Chapter 6 STRATEGY   75
Chapter 7 TOLERATION   79
Chapter 8 REMAINING SURE   88
Chapter 9 JUSTIFICATION   102
Chapter 10 CONFIRMATION   114
Chapter 11 FOUNDATIONS   123
Chapter 12 PERCEPTION   136
Chapter 13 ACCESS TO TRUTH   152
Chapter 14 CONCLUSION   159
NOTES   162

NAME INDEX   169
SUBJECT INDEX   170

Introduction

The following inquiry has two main objectives. The first is to describe an ideal form of the knowledge of truth, the second to defend the view that such an ideal is realistic. It goes without saying that knowledge is worthwhile, both as a means and as an end. But some forms are intrinsically more desirable than others, and the first task is to find the most desirable form. There is an important constraint on the search, however. The question of whether we have such knowledge must be left open. The ideal should not be set so high that it is clearly unattainable nor so low that its realization is trivial.

Describing knowledge is not just a matter of describing ordinary usage, since plain men rarely, if ever, use "knowledge" in an ideal sense. The task is partly one of constructing a suitable concept. Yet there cannot be a complete break from ordinary usage. The ideal should bear some relationship to what we have in mind when we first ask philosophical questions about knowledge. Although ordinary concepts can be reshaped, they should not be entirely replaced.

Establishing that the ideal is realistic involves opposing a sceptic in the sense of someone who disclaims ideal knowledge on distinctively philosophical grounds. His grounds can be as mundane as facts about sense experience, provided he uses a philosophical argument to disclose their significance. He can therefore allow knowledge as long as he limits it for philosophical reasons. And he is free to allow less ideal forms of knowledge. Granted, the concept of a philosophical reason may not always be easy to apply. But this simply means that the concept of a sceptic has rough edges. Since there are potentially clear cases, the concept is sharp enough for our purposes.

The task of constructing an ideal concept is undertaken in part I. The materials are assembled in the first four chapters and the concept constructed in the fifth. Part II contains the apologetic response to scepticism. The strategy that it adopts will be discussed in chapter 6.

PART I
The Concept of Knowledge

CHAPTER ONE

Plausibility

1. A MINIMAL CONCEPT

The first thing we need is a concept that belongs to the same general category as concepts like "reasonable," "justified," or "probable," but that is far less demanding. Indeed, we need a concept the application of which is compatible with the application of any other concept from the same category, including negative concepts like "unjustified" and "improbable." In this sense, we need a *minimal* epistemic concept.

Let us use "plausible" to express the desired concept. Ordinarily, the word is used to make a limited claim. But it is probably never used to make a minimal claim. For instance, although a conjecture can in an ordinary sense be both plausible and unproven, it cannot be both plausible and certainly false. Yet both combinations are possible in the technical sense. The technical concept has no place in ordinary thought because normally we want to locate even our conjectures as far along the epistemic road as we can. Plausibility therefore has little, if any, practical significance. But it *is* theoretically important.[1]

Consider a case in which a witness in a murder trial testifies that the defendant did commit the murder. The testimony makes it plausible to think that the defendant is the murderer. Now suppose that subsequent testimony indicates that the witness is a habitual liar, that he is prejudiced against the defendant, and that the witness himself had opportunity and motive to commit the crime. The witness's testimony then seems worthless. But the belief that the defendant committed the murder is still technically plausible. In other words, testimony confers plausibility independently of any further considerations, whereas the worth of that testimony depends upon further considerations. Thus, if still further testimony indicates that the testimony that purports to discredit the witness is itself worthless, the witness's testimony can help support a guilty verdict. This is how the concept of plausibility remains minimal. Further developments might make something that is plausible certainly true or, on the other hand, they might make it certainly false. Its being plausible is compatible with either result.

Some might have difficulty with this notion of independence. Why, they might ask, should we say that the witness's testimony confers plausibility on the defendant's guilt even when the testimony is discredited? Why not say that the defendant's guilt fails to be plausible when the witness's testimony is completely worthless?

There are two reasons for not adopting such a recommendation. First, a jury that hears the witness can thereupon find the defendant's guilt plausible without having to hear any further testimony. This does not mean that the jury can thereupon arrive at a responsible verdict. Far from it. But the jury can say that the prosecution does have an opening move. And it is theoretically important to preserve this concept of an opening move. Second, even if further developments do discredit the witness, the fact that those developments might in turn be discredited by still further considerations suggests that we should not make everything that testimony confers on a proposition a function of further considerations. There does seem to be something about the relationship between the witness's testimony and the defendant's guilt that is not a function of whether discrediting testimony is undermined by further testimony, whether the latter is undermined by still further testimony, and so on. Indeed, there seems to be something about the relationship that is not a function of any further considerations, and "confers plausibility" is intended to capture that feature.

Plausibility is therefore distinct from probability, both in a sense in which probability contrasts with improbability and in a sense in which probability ranges on a scale from 0.0 to 1.0. For example, if someone assures us that Martians will invade earth next year, the invasion is plausible but highly improbable. Or if I seem to see a magician vanish into thin air, his vanishing is plausible, even though it is impossible. The zero probability of the magician's vanishing is a function of further considerations, whereas the plausibility of his vanishing is the simple product of my seeming to see what I do. Since plausibility is compatible with both improbability and zero probability, it remains suitably minimal.

2. EVIDENCE

There is a sense of "evidence" in which evidence and plausibility
are closely connected. The mere presence of testimony establishes plausibility and, more generally, the mere presence of evidence has the same result. Even if evidence turns out to be bad in
light of further evidence, it can still confer plausibility. Of course,
ordinary language is not always sensitive to the distinction between evidence and bad evidence. It would not be eccentric to
say that the disreputable witness's testimony is not evidence at all
once it has been discredited, meaning that it should not be relied
on at all. But we can make the same point by saying that the
testimony is thoroughly bad evidence, and in this sense evidence
is closely linked to plausibility.

Even so, preserving a close link involves taking some liberties
with ordinary usage. If we do say that anything that confers
plausibility on p is evidence in favour of $p,$ we have to include a
deductive form of evidence. Moreover, since evidence that discloses a possibility also confers plausibility, we must say that
evidence that indicates that something *may* be the case is evidence it *is* the case. For example, frequency evidence that a long
run of heads is possible is then evidence that the run will occur.
Similarly, since something impossible can be plausible, evidence
that makes it plausible to think that a magician has vanished is
then evidence that the magician has vanished. These are slightly
odd uses of "evidence." But they do not distort the concept beyond recognition.

A similar connection might be thought to hold between plausibility and an epistemic reason for belief. Hypnosis and insecurity
are in a sense reasons for belief. But they are not epistemic reasons, unlike someone's remembering something. And we might
say that if it is plausible to believe $p,$ there is epistemic reason to
believe $p,$ bearing in mind that reasons can be good or bad. Thus,
just as the disreputable witness's testimony is bad evidence of the
defendant's guilt, so it affords a bad reason to believe that he
committed the murder.

The resulting impositions on ordinary usage are harder to accept in this case, however. For example, we must then say that if
an observed frequency establishes the possibility, and hence the
plausibility, of a long run of heads, it affords a reason to believe
that a long run will occur, not merely that it may occur. Similarly,

we must say that there is reason to believe that the magician has vanished. Even if we quickly add that the reason is a bad one, the remark still seems offensive.

We can circumvent this difficulty by linking plausibility simply with a reason for having an affirmative attitude. Attitudes form a continuous spectrum, with conviction falling at or near one end, indifference in the centre, and complete rejection at or near the other end. We can say that something is plausible if, and only if, there is reason to adopt an affirmative attitude toward it, where such an attitude can fall as close to indifference as one chooses. Thus, if getting a long run of heads is barely possible in a given situation, there is on that account reason to adopt an affirmative attitude toward "A long run will occur," although there is no reason to believe the proposition. Similarly, there is reason to adopt an affirmative attitude toward "The magician has vanished," although the reason is thoroughly bad. In this way, we can maintain the minimal character of plausibility.

3. DISTINGUISHING MARKS

We can strengthen our grip on the concept of plausibility by considering the following distinguishing features.

There are no degrees or amounts of plausibility, since the notion of something's having a greater minimal standing than something else is incoherent. In an ordinary sense, of course, we can say that one supposition is more plausible than another, meaning that there is a greater presumption of truth in the one case, or that the evidence on hand currently favours one over the other. But such ordinary judgments take into account a body of evidence, albeit of an incomplete sort, and therefore they are not minimal judgments.

Granted, one thing can be plausible in more respects than another. For example, one thing can be reported by more witnesses. Nevertheless, although increasing the number of supporting witnesses can improve a position, it does not improve things by increasing the position's plausibility. It improves things by reducing the chance that the given testimony is unreliable. Thus, multiplying witnesses does not make a position more plausible. It makes the testimony more reliable. Just one witness is enough to make the position plausible, which is as plausible as any position can be.

Plausibility can attach to inconsistent propositions. Frequency evidence that indicates that a long run of heads is possible, though improbable, confers plausibility on both "A long run will occur" and "A long run will not occur." Similarly, one proposition is both plausible and implausible if it is affirmed by one person and denied by another. Even a self-contradictory proposition is plausible if it is affirmed by someone. Such results will seem paradoxical only if we forget the special minimal nature of plausibility. Saying that a contradiction is plausible is not to commend it. The remark merely establishes a precondition of commendation that can be conjoined with a subsequent condemnation. For instance, we can say, "It is plausible to think that something can be at a distance from itself, because Russell defended such a contingency; but the view is false," having argued that Russell's defence fails to work.

Plausibility is nonconjunctive, in the sense that a conjunction of individually plausible propositions need not itself be plausible. For example, one person can affirm a proposition and another deny it, where no one affirms the conjunction of the two. Granted, plausibility is transferred through deduction, in the sense that the plausibility of p $(p \vdash q)$ yields the plausibility of q. But if the deduction involves more than one premise, plausibility is not transferred unless the conjunction of the premises is plausible.

Plausibility is temporal, in the sense that something can be plausible at one time and not at another. For example, suppose that a witness's report makes something plausible, the witness dies, no one remembers the report, no one else witnessed the incident, and no record is kept. The incident then ceases to be plausible. Ignoring any requirements imposed by divine omniscience, plausibility is not an eternal possession. Granted, some propositions (e.g., "$2 + 2 = 4$") might be endlessly plausible. But even they seem capable of ceasing to be plausible if there were no intelligent beings to consider them. At any rate, it is hard to see how we could ever show that they would then still be plausible.

Plausibility is not subjective, in the sense that it is not a simple function of how we find things to be. This point involves a subtle distinction, since someone's finding something plausible is enough to make it plausible. The point is that there is a conceptual distinction between saying that something is plausible and saying that it is found to be plausible. As a result, it is possible for someone to find something plausible because of what he remembers and for it not to be plausible because of anything he remembers, although it is plausible because he finds it plausible. For example, suppose that someone remembers that all A's are B's and that x is B, mistakenly thinks that a universal affirmative proposition is convertible, and as a result finds it plausible that x is A. He is mistaken to the extent that "x is A" is not plausible for his reasons, although it is plausible because he finds it plausible.

Plausibility is not objective, in the sense that it is not dependent on truth, reality, real events, or actual states of affairs. For instance, it can be plausible to think that Socrates both died and failed to die, even though it is not true that he both died and failed to die, and even though the two conflicting states of affairs did not actually obtain. Conversely, it is possible for the proposition "A purple planet existed billions of years before earth" to be true and yet never to be plausible. The latter point holds for logically necessary truths as well as for contingent truths. Granted, I cannot reasonably cite an example of a possible nonplausible necessary truth. A possible necessary truth must be necessary, and I cannot reasonably say that something is necessary unless I find it plausible. But I can coherently imagine what things would have been like if a necessary truth that is plausible in our world had not been plausible at all.

Although plausibility is independent of truth and reality, plausibility can be attached to "things" as well as to beliefs, statements, conjectures, etc. We can say that it is plausible that London is in England, as well as saying that it is plausible to think as much and that the corresponding belief is plausible. Indeed, we can even say that London's being in England is plausible, and refer to the plausibility of such a state of affairs. This may mark a significant departure from ordinary usage. But that simply indicates how special the technical concept is. It does not reveal a conceptual flaw.

Some might think that assigning plausibility to things implies the existence of nonreal entities, since plausibility claims are admittedly independent of reality. Now, it is true that we are committed to saying that there are plausible states of affairs, where such states need not actually obtain. But this does not mean that we are thereby committed to saying that such states are *entities*. When we refer to states of affairs without presupposing that they actually obtain, we do not have to presuppose that they have a special kind of existence. We do have to say that there are such states. But if calling them "entities" means nothing more than this, the result is harmless. On the other hand, if calling them "entities" goes significantly further—as it normally does—the metaphysical commitment needs to be established. If it cannot be established, no harm results. If it can be established, the reasons for accepting the commitment are also reasons for not finding the commitment harmful. Consequently, either way the metaphysical objection is unfounded.

Thus, someone who denies that states of affairs are entities can consistently assign plausibility to such states. Of course, someone who refuses to say that there are states of affairs cannot go this far. But his position is too extreme, since in no sense can he then say that there are things of which he denies the existence, viz., states of affairs. His position becomes attractive only if it is confused with a legitimate worry about treating states of affairs as entities.

4. INTUITIVE PLAUSIBILITY

Some things are plausible because something else is plausible. For example, it is plausible that Locke read Aristotle because Locke refers to Aristotle in the *Essay* and normally philosophers read the authors to whom they refer. On the other hand, some things are plausible without being plausible because something else is plausible. For example, it is plausible that $2 + 2 = 4$ quite apart from whether anyone asserts the equation or finds it plausible. The equation is simply plausible on its own. Call the first kind of plausibility *derivative* and the second kind *intuitive*. Also, call someone's finding something intuitively plausible an *intuition*.

Intuitive and derivative plausibility are not exclusive, since intuitively plausible propositions can be deduced from other plausible propositions. Moreover, something intuitively plausible can be derivatively implausible, since someone can find something implausible when it is intuitively plausible. Indeed, the only unacceptable combination is something's being both intuitively plausible and intuitively implausible. If something is plausible on its own, it cannot also be implausible on its own.

Some philosophers are reluctant to give a word like "intuition" a prominent role in their epistemology. But in this context the word avoids the associations that give rise to such suspicions.

For example, an intuition is not regarded as the outcome of examining abstract entities. If someone intuits that $2 + 2 = 4$, there is something he find intuitively plausible, viz. $2 + 2 = 4$.

But as we have seen, we need not assume that "what there is" is always an entity. Nor, therefore, need we assume that a constituent of what someone finds plausible—such as the number 2—is an entity.

Intuition does not involve the use of a special intellectual or inner sense. Someone who intuits that he feels pain is not relying on such a sense, in the way that someone who finds it plausible to believe that he is holding a pen relies on his tactile and visual senses. Indeed, someone who had to rely on an inner sense would find it plausible to believe that he feels pain *because* of what he senses with his inner eye. And in that case he would not find the belief intuitively plausible. Perceptual models of intuition are therefore incoherent. Consequently, we should resist the temptation to characterize intuition as a case of intellectual apprehension or introspective awareness.

Intuitive plausibility is not the same as self-evidence. Understood in one way, a self-evident proposition is one about which we cannot be mistaken, whereas we can be mistaken about an intuitively plausible proposition. For instance, people are frequently mistaken about intuitively plausible truth-functional tautologies. Moreover, they often find something intuitively plausible when it is not; e.g., I once mistakenly found propositions like 'I am sensing a red sense datum' intuitively plausible.

Understood in another way, a self-evident proposition is one we are justified in accepting independently of any further considerations. But we can correctly intuit something without being justified in accepting it. For example, we need not be justified if our intuition is unclear, or if someone with impressive credentials disagrees with us, or if we have a history of abandoned intuitions. Intuitions are not weapons that can be used to club opponents into submission, even when the intuitions are correct. An intuition is therefore quite unlike Locke's immediate perception of the agreement or disagreement of ideas. For Locke, such a perception is a sufficient condition of having intuitive knowledge, whereas intuition is merely a necessary condition.[2]

An intuitively plausible proposition need not be true, and an intuitively plausible state of affairs need not actually obtain. For example, my feeling pain can be intuitively plausible even though I do not actually feel pain. Granted, this means that, logically, a state of affairs can fail to obtain even though there is no way for us to tell that it does. But there is no reason to think that we cannot coherently decide to use our terms in a way that leaves room for such a possibility.

Critics of intuitive starting points often have their sights fixed on something other than intuitive plausibility. For instance, Lehrer rejects beliefs that are "completely justified in themselves without need of any independent information"; Williams rejects "intrinsically credible" beliefs in the sense of beliefs that belong to a class with predominantly true members; and Armstrong rejects "initially credible" beliefs in the sense of beliefs that need only be true in order to be known.[3] Intuitively plausible beliefs are not justified in themselves. They are simply plausible in themselves. Nor is it logically necessary that most intuitively plausible beliefs are true. And adding truth to intuitive plausibility is not enough to yield knowledge. For example, a student who correctly intuits the negation of a professor's statement need not know the negation even if it is true. The student might not be justified in accepting the negation because of the professor's stature.

Granted, there is a necessary connection between something's being intuitively plausible and its being certain. Any ground for adopting a negative attitude toward an intuitively plausible proposition is worthless, in which case the proposition is certain. For example, if 'It is possible for some men to be short and others tall' is intuitively plausible, the intuitions that give rise to a sorites argument in favour of 'All men must be short if any man is' cannot all be sound. No objection can be sound as long as what it tries to overthrow really is intuitively plausible.

Nevertheless, the link between intuitive plausibility and certainty does not alter any of the foregoing points. As we shall see in chapter 3, certainty is independent of truth and justification. Moreover, we can rarely appeal to intuitive plausibility in order to demonstrate certainty, since someone will rarely accept an intuition that he does not share.

True, this means that if nothing is certain, nothing is intuitively plausible. Anyone who disclaims certainty should therefore also reject intuitive plausibility. But such a result is not unwelcome. Whether the rejection is sound then depends upon the merit of the sceptic's reasons for disclaiming certainty. I am not trying to outline a concept of intuitive plausibility that is unarguably applicable. I merely want one that is not patently *in*applicable.

The connection between intuitive plausibility and certainty might seem to create the following problem. Imagine that the pain possession report "I have pain in an arm" is intuitively plausible and hence certain. It is also intuitively plausible that "I have pain in an arm" entails the arm report, "I have an arm." Consequently, the arm report is certain. But in a phantom-limb case this result seems absurd. Not only does the amputee lack an arm, it also seems certain that he lacks one.

Such a result can be avoided by noting that there are really two possession reports and two arm reports. The intuitively plausible possession report is one entailed by "I feel pain in an arm," and the arm report entailed by this possession report is not about a public arm. Consequently, this arm report is not certainly false in a phantom-limb case. On the other hand, the arm report that is certainly false implies the existence of a public arm. It is entailed by a possession report that is not entailed by "I feel pain in an arm." Thus, the same arm report is not both certain and certainly false. (The notion of an arm report that is not about a public arm receives further attention in chapter 12, in a discussion of the things we perceive.)

Finally, carving out a concept of intuitive plausibility is not to attach it exclusively to a specific kind of state of affair, belief, or proposition. Those who distrust assigning epistemic priority to just one kind of proposition should not on that account reject intuitive plausibility.

5. DERIVATIVE PLAUSIBILITY

Sources of plausibility are highly varied. They can be deductive, as in

> If it is plausible both that p and that p entails q, it is plausible that q.

or nondeductive, as in

> If it is plausible that someone testifies (observes, remembers, judges) that p, it is plausible that p.

> If it is plausible that somebody immediately perceives something $\emptyset$, it is plausible that an $\emptyset$ object exists.

> If it is plausible that $n\%$ of observed A's are $\emptyset$, it is plausible that $n\%$ of A's are $\emptyset$.

> If it is plausible that some A's are $\emptyset$, it is plausible that the next A will be $\emptyset$.

> If it is plausible that S had a motive for doing a, it is plausible that S did a.

> If it is plausible that x existed at time t and also existed at a later time t', it is plausible that x existed from t to t'.

Such conditions belong to a set of plausibility principles, although there is no reason to think that this list exhausts the set. Indeed, there is no reason to think that the set is finite.

Plausibility principles are in a sense rules of evidence, provided we use "evidence" in the rather distinctive way sketched in section 2 of this chapter. We must remember, however, that they only concern plausibility, unlike some of the principles that philosophers have in mind when they talk of rules of evidence. For example, Russell offers a more ambitious rule when he says: "My recollecting confers some credibility on what is recollected."[4] He makes credibility vary in degree, assimilates degree of credibility to degree of antecedent probability, and, in the case of memory, proportions degree of credibility to the degree of accuracy of previous memories. Similarly, Price goes farther when he suggests that an object's being perceptually presented is *prima facie* evidence of the object's existence. *Prima facie* evidence entitles us to presume that an object exists, whereas the plausibility of an object's existing does not warrant even a presumption.[5]

Critics of rules of evidence also tend to have more ambitious principles in mind. For example, Williams holds that someone with independent reason to distrust his senses can justifiably say that his sensing red affords no reason to suppose that a red material object exists.[6] Now, it is true that his sensing red affords no *good* reason in such circumstances. Moreover, it does not afford even a bad reason to *suppose* that a red material object does exist. But it does afford a bad reason for adopting an affirmative attitude toward the material-object proposition, an attitude that the person should not adopt precisely because the reason is a bad one. Indeed, otherwise the question of the reliability of his senses would not arise. Harman similarly argues that rules of evidence are unfortunately designed to underwrite the "claim that certain evidence provides a good reason to believe a particular conclusion."[7] Plausibility principles do not describe conditions of there being good reasons for belief. Plausibility principles merely describe conditions of there being reasons for adopting an affirmative attitude. Whether the reasons are any good, and whether the attitude should be one of belief, is another matter.

When correct, plausibility principles are necessary truths. They are also *a priori,* in the sense that they do not draw their plausibility from what we observe. But, contrary to what Lehrer suggests, this does not make them "binding on all men and all epistemology."[8] If they are correct, men should abide by them in the course of making plausibility judgments. But not all men will. And there is ample room for debating their correctness. For example, not everyone will agree that plausibility can be derived from sensory evidence, and this issue can, and should, be pursued. The fact that a principle is necessary and *a priori* does not rule out such an investigation.

Plausibility principles are therefore not analytic in any sense that implies that they cannot be sensibly denied without altering the meanings of the words involved. For example, we might contest the principle

> If it is plausible that a person grimaces, it is plausible that he feels pain.

on the ground that grimacing is a piece of learned pain behavior. The objection may be mistaken, but it need not betray an ignorance of what "pain" or "grimace" mean. Nor need it involve an unconscious attempt to change their meaning. Similarly, we might reject the principle on the ground that grimacing does not entail feeling pain, because we fail to notice that the necessary connection is between the plausibility of the given propositions and not between the propositions themselves.

Although plausibility principles are themselves intuitively plausible and hence certain, they are not on that account unarguable. Sometimes our intuitions are too feeble or fleeting to justify accepting a principle. Sometimes criticisms are so vigorous that even a clear and firm intuition is not enough to justify acceptance. And even if we are justified in being sure of a principle, there is still room to debate whether the principle really is intuitively plausible. Consequently, the intuitive plausibility of plausibility principles is no obstacle to their being subjects of free inquiry.

6. SUMMARY

The technical concept of plausibility is intelligible, coherent, and free of gratuitous metaphysical assumptions. Mastering it particularly involves understanding the features that make it a minimal concept. This is doubly important, since those features also protect its intuitive and derivative forms from difficulties that plague more familiar counterparts. For example, intuitive plausibility is less demanding than self-evidence, and deriving plausibility is easier than deriving a degree of justification.

Plausibility will eventually be used to explain certainty, which in turn will be used to explain knowledge. But before we discuss certainty, we should first look at probability.

Probability

1. INTRODUCTION

It will be helpful at the outset to stipulate three general features of probability.

First, although probability allows comparisons, it contrasts with improbability. Hence any mathematical value should exceed 0.5.

Second, something probable can be certain and hence have a value of 1.0. Thus, "It is probable that p" does not entail "It may be that not p"—i.e., the contrary of something probable can be impossible in an epistemic sense.

Third, something probable need not be true. A horse can be the probable winner of a racé without being the actual winner. This means that "It is probable that p" is not a tentative assertion that p. It is a claim about what the evidence is like with respect to p. Granted, the conjunction "It is probable that p, and it is false that p" is odd. But the oddness is akin to that of the self-refuting "p, and I don't believe that p." It does not show that making probability independent of truth is incoherent.

Two things follow from separating probability from truth. Probability is then independent of logically necessary truth, which means that tautologies need not have a value of 1.0, or contradictions a value of 0.0. Moreover, probability is then not an indeterministic counterpart of causal necessity. A high incidence of $\varnothing$'s among A's can in a sense make it probable that the next A will be $\varnothing$, regardless of whether there is evidence of the incidence. But I am deliberately not using "probable" in that sense in the present context. Probability requires evidence, simply by *fiat*. To this extent probability is not a matter of objective chance.

Within the above limitations, two senses of "probability" are especially important for our purposes. In one sense, probability has certainty as a limiting case. In another, probability is involved in the justification of certainty claims. I shall call the two, respectively, *absolute* probability and *relative* probability.

2. RELATIVE PROBABILITY

Relative probability is the product of two conditions—plausibility and the absence of preponderant counterevidence—where both conditions are satisfied strictly in relation to given evidence. Thus, something that satisfies conditions of probability for one body of evidence need not do so for another. For example, a probable winner before a race can be a probable loser afterward.

The given evidence to which probability is relativized can take different shapes. For instance, it can be a specific piece of evidence—as in "Given that most regulations have been obeyed, this one will probably also be obeyed"—or a selection of someone's evidence—as in "Given what occurs to me offhand, that's probable"—or someone's total evidence at a given time; or someone's evidence over a short period of time; or the evidence of a scientific community at a given time; or the evidence that a community either has or can easily acquire; or the evidence had by everyone at a given time.

For our purposes, the best frame of reference is a person's total evidence at a given time. Ultimately, we want to describe a form of knowledge that incorporates a personal ideal. This involves identifying the conditions of an individual's having knowledge at a given time. It is therefore potentially useful to shape other epistemic concepts along the same individualistic lines.

The reference to a given time may seem problematic. If the time is a period, the question "How short?" arises. If the time is unextended, there is a question of whether having evidence at a time is even possible. To avoid such problems, let us understand "so and so's evidence at t" to include any evidence he has prior to t that he does not stop having at or before t, and any evidence that he starts to have at t. This makes the temporal reference instantaneous, yet it restricts instants to the termini of periods of possession.

The notion of evidence-possession needs sharpening. Let us say that someone has evidence that p if, and only if, he either correctly finds something plausible from which p's plausibility is derivable, or such a source is plausible and he would have found it so had he considered the matter, other things being equal. This means that if someone finds a potential source of p's plausibility intuitively plausible and the source is not intuitively plausible, he does not have evidence that p. It also means that someone who sees a flash on a radar screen does not have evidence of an approaching aircraft unless he has suitable background information. Moreover, it means that, even if someone thinks that p's plausibility is not derivable from what he finds plausible, he can still have evidence that p if p's plausibility *is* so derivable. For example, someone can have evidence of a friend's reputation and yet refuse to acknowledge it because of envy.

The account provides for cases where someone does not actually find a source plausible but would have done so upon consideration. For example, someone can have evidence by observing something, even though he does not find his observing it plausible. It is enough that he would have found his observation plausible had he considered the matter. But this does not mean that someone can acquire evidence that p merely by, say, buying a book that contains evidence that p. Although he would have found a source plausible had he read the book, he would not have found a source plausible had he simply considered the matter, other things remaining equal. Adding the counterfactual option does loosen the range of the concept of evidence-possession. But it does not make the concept vacuous.

We are using "evidence" in the broad plausibility-conferring sense discussed in section 2 of chapter 1. The term "counterevidence" will be used even more broadly, to include not only something that confers implausibility, but also something that discredits a source of plausibility, something that confers implausibility on a source of plausibility, and so on. For example, imagine that John testifies that p and Mary testifies that not p. Mary's evidence is then counterevidence with respect to p. Now imagine that Mary also testifies that John is an habitual liar. This part of her testimony is also counterevidence, although it does not make p implausible. Rather, it discredits John's testimony. Imagine as well that Peter testifies that John is really not testifying that p. This too is counterevidence, although in this instance it tries to eliminate John's testimony entirely.

We shall also say that there is counterevidence with respect to p if p is intuitively implausible.

Whether counterevidence is preponderant depends upon two factors: first, whether it is discredited; second, whether it has greater or equal weight. For example, suppose that a journalist argues that urbanization has not harmed the nuclear family in the United States, and in his support he cites countries with large cities and healthy families. Suppose that a sociologist replies that the theory attacked by the journalist presupposes enabling conditions that are not present in the cited countries. Suppose that a second sociologist attacks the journalist's qualifications as a researcher and refuses to accept his premise. Suppose that a third sociologist discloses that the cited countries are all populated by individuals who are radically unlike Americans in their attitudes toward the family. Finally, suppose that a fourth sociologist is otherwise satisfied but cites many more countries in which urbanization correlates with the family's breakdown. If the first sociologist is right, the journalist has provided no counterevidence. If the second and third sociologists are right, the journalist has provided *bad* counterevidence, since the support for his premise is discredited and the premise itself is also discredited as evidence for the conclusion. If the fourth sociologist is right, the journalist has provided *slight* counterevidence, since even though the journalist does offer counterevidence and it does have some weight, it is outweighed by further considerations. Thus, preponderant counterevidence must be neither bad nor slight.

We can now say, with slightly more precision, that something is *relatively probable* given someone's total evidence if, and only if, (a) it is plausible given his evidence, and (b) his evidence contains no preponderant counterevidence. Thus something has a maximum degree of relative probability if it is plausible given someone's evidence and his evidence contains no good counterevidence. The degree falls short of the maximum if his evidence contains counterevidence that has some weight, decreasing as the weight of his counterevidence increases.

3. THE SIGNIFICANCE OF RELATIVE PROBABILITY

Some may find the notion of relative probability useless, on the ground that we can never know what someone's total evidence is, even in our own case. In particular, they may feel that we can never know whether our evidence is free of preponderant counterevidence.[1]

Now, it is true that we can never know what our total evidence is, in the sense that we can never knowingly articulate it all. It may even be true that we can never in this sense know what our total relevant evidence is. But this does not mean that we can never know that our evidence contains supporting evidence and no preponderant counterevidence. Our intuitions can come to our rescue in this connection. For example, I find it intuitively plausible that I have media evidence that Canada will face serious oil shortages by 1990. I also find it intuitively plausible that I have no preponderant counterevidence in this regard, even though I cannot describe all my information that might have a bearing on the question. Assuming that knowledge of any sort is possible, this enables me to know that relative to my evidence Canada will probably have oil shortages by 1990.

Granted, such intuitions are fallible. Someone might point out grounds for optimism concerning the oil situation, grounds with which I was perfectly familiar but that escaped my notice when I originally assessed my evidence. Yet this does not mean that our intuitions are never correct, or that intuitions concerning our evidence are so unreliable that they can never be sources of knowledge. It simply means that in any given situation we may fail to have the knowledge of probability that we think we have—which is an acceptable result.

A relative-probability claim fits the requirements of a logical theory, of the sort offered by Keynes and Carnap.[2] Appraising a relative claim involves determining whether a complete description of given evidence logically implies that the conditions of probability are satisfied. If the claim "p is probable given evidence e" is correct, a complete description of e contains no preponderant counterevidence. Admittedly, we can never give a complete description of e for a reasonably developed human mind. But we can still estimate whether a complete description would have such implications.

This does not mean that a relative probability claim is too subjective to permit error. A claim can be mistaken about the particular contents of given evidence. Or it can be wrong about whether given evidence satisfies the requirements of probability. Or it can be wrong about the degree of probability. There is no need to identify something's having a probability relative to given evidence with someone's thinking that it does. Even relative probability is to this extent objective.

There is one feature of relative probability that severely limits its epistemological significance, however. Expanding the evidence to which a claim is relativized cannot make the resulting claim any better. Even if the two claims are opposed, they can both be equally correct.[3] Moreover, the correctness of a claim indicates nothing about the consequences of expanding the given evidence. As a result, relative-probability claims are quite distinct from knowledge claims.

For example, suppose that before a horse race x is the probable winner, and just after the race y is. Both probability claims are correct and, from the standpoint of relative probability, the second one is no better than the first. Moreover, nothing in either probability claim indicates what the result of adding further evidence will be. Thus, an hour after the end of the race, evidence of a disqualification might make it probable that z is the winner. Now, suppose that before the race we claim to know that x will be the winner, and then, just after the race, we claim to know that y was the winner, and then, after hearing of the disqualification, we claim to know that z was the winner. Although our claims can all be justified, there does seem to be an *epistemic* respect in which they are not all equal. That is, it is not merely that one of the three horses is the real winner. Moreover, the prerace claim to know that x will win implies that developments that favour another horse will not subsequently occur. Consequently, to capture the full epistemic dimensions of knowledge, we need something other than relative probability.

4. ABSOLUTE PROBABILITY

Suppose that we introduce another concept of probability by modifying the requirement that demands the absence of preponderant counterevidence. Instead of saying that a given person's evidence will *contain* no preponderant counterevidence, let us say that there will *be* none, at any time and regardless of who has it. We thus continue to make probability a function of someone's total evidence by continuing to make the plausibility requirement depend on it. In this respect the resulting probability is not absolute. But we also make probability less relative by making the second requirement depend upon what all the evidence is like. It is a demand on the *absolutely total evidence,* not just on someone's total evidence. In this respect the resulting probability *is* absolute.

Accordingly, let us say that something is *absolutely probable* given someone's total evidence if, and only if, (i) it is plausible given his evidence, and (ii) there is no preponderant counterevidence in the absolutely total evidence.

Absolute probability is not so absolute that something probable at one time cannot fail to be probable at another time. For example, we can suppose that at 10 A.M., May 1, 1660, it was plausible, given Spinoza's evidence, that Spinoza was grinding lenses, but that this was not plausible given Russell's evidence at 10 A.M., May 1, 1960. The claim that Spinoza was probably grinding lenses on May 1, 1660, can then be correct given Spinoza's evidence, whereas it cannot be correct given Russell's evidence. Moreover, a change in the plausibility source can produce a different result. Thus, imagine that Russell's evidence does indicate that Spinoza was grinding lenses at the appropriate time, because Russell remembers having read a suitable diary entry. If there is preponderant evidence discrediting the diary, an absolute probability claim is still incorrect given Russell's evidence, whereas it can be correct given Spinoza's evidence, since Spinoza was not relying on a diary entry.

On the other hand, if the plausibility requirement is uniformly satisfied, opposing claims cannot both be correct. It is then a question of what the absolutely total evidence is like, not of what someone's evidence is like, and there can only be one right answer to this question. For example, if Spinoza and Russell both rely on the same diary entry, then, if an absolute claim is correct given Spinoza's evidence, it must also be correct given Russell's evidence.

This means that there is room for improvement in claiming absolute probability. For one thing, if a claim that is made in light of someone's evidence turns out to be wrong when his evidence is augmented, the claim was wrong right from the start. For example, imagine that someone claims that nuclear energy stations will probably never have a major accident, because he remembers having read several authoritative accounts of the safety precautions adopted at nuclear stations. Imagine that he continues to remember what he read, but then hears of the near disaster in Pennsylvania. If his probability claim is no longer correct because what he now hears affords preponderant counterevidence, the claim was incorrect when he first made it. Even then the absolutely total evidence contained preponderant counterevidence. The claim "Probably there will be a major accident" is the better claim right from the start.

Moreover, although opposing probability claims can both be correct, in the sense that "It is probable that p" can be correct given one person's evidence and "It is not probable that p" can be correct given another person's evidence, claims that assert the probability of opposing states of affairs cannot both be correct. For example, imagine that Russell's evidence makes it plausible that Spinoza was not grinding lenses on May 1, 1660. The fact that the absolutely total evidence contains no preponderant counterevidence with respect to Spinoza's evidence that he was grinding means that it has to contain preponderant counterevidence with respect to Russell's evidence that Spinoza was not grinding.

An absolute probability claim does imply something about future evidence, since it implies that there is no preponderant counterevidence in the absolutely total evidence, which includes all future evidence. This feature will no doubt produce concern, since some will feel that we can never justifiably imply such a thing, that we can never tell what evidence the future will bring. But it is not obvious that such claims cannot be justified, as I shall argue in chapter 9. And the fact that they do attract sceptical attention is a reason for constructing them and being prepared to defend them.

Absolute probability is not adequately described by familiar theories of probability.[4] It is independent of actual states of affairs or events, contrary to an objective-chance theory. Sophisticated mistakes about absolute probability are possible, contrary to a subjective theory that identifies the probable with educated betting preferences. Moreover, absolute probability resists a logical account. A complete description of someone's evidence at a given time cannot entail anything about the same person's evidence at another time, or about someone else's evidence. Hence it cannot entail that there is no preponderant counterevidence in the absolutely total evidence. Thus, as a measure of absolute probability, the formula $Pr(p, e) = n$ is not a necessary truth if e is someone's total evidence at a given time.

This does not mean that we must define absolute probability in terms of relative frequency. Single-case claims are not frequency claims. The claim that Ontario universities will probably suffer declining enrolments through the 1980's is not a claim about observed frequencies, although it can be based on frequency evidence. Moreover, the general claim "Probably most A's are $\emptyset$" is not a projection of the long-run frequency of $\emptyset A$'s among observed A's. Granted, the claim does imply, and in this sense means, that in appropriate circumstances most observed A's will continue to be $\emptyset$—i.e., that the observed frequency will suitably converge above 0.5 in the long run. But the claim carries this implication because otherwise there would be preponderant evidence for saying that most A's are not $\emptyset$. The implication is not because the claim *asserts* that the long-run observed frequency will have such a pattern. For instance, the claim also implies that

there will be no authentic divine revelation that most A's are not
$\emptyset$. But it does not assert anything about divine revelation. Frequency theories tend to be insensitive to this distinction.

Absolute probability is not just a matter of the ratio of favourable to total possibilities. Possibilities can be strictly relative to
someone's total evidence. For example, if someone is told that a
given die is unbiased and he has no evidence of bias, each side of
the die is an equal possibility on his evidence, in which case there
is a classical probability that a non-6 will be tossed. Yet if there is
further evidence that the die has been loaded to toss 6, there is no
absolute probability that a non-6 will be tossed. Classical theories
tend to obscure this fact.

5. INDIFFERENCE

A principle of indifference can play a limited role in determining
absolute probabilities. Some would hesitate to go so far, arguing
that indifference principles are bound to generate contradictions
when applied to cases of extreme ignorance. For example, imagine that the only thing we know about a die-tossing situation is
that one side will turn up. A useful principle says that if there is
no good reason for preferring any alternative in an exhaustive set,
each alternative is equally possible. Consequently, the principle
can seem to imply that, since we are given no reason to prefer any
of the six possible tosses, each toss is equally possible, in which
case tossing a non-6 is probable. Yet the principle can also seem
to imply that, since we are given no reason to prefer a non-6 over
a 6, each of these alternatives is equally possible, in which case
tossing a non-6 is not probable.

The apparent contradiction results from transforming our ignorance about the case into a condition about what the evidence in
the case is like.[5] If we are given nothing about the case except
that each side is an alternative, we cannot apply the principle at
all. The principle works for absolute probability only if it says
that alternatives are equipossible if there is no good reason for
preference in the absolutely total evidence. If we are not told
whether the latter condition is satisfied by the evidence, we cannot apply the principle. On the other hand, if we are given that
there is no reason in the absolutely total evidence for preferring
any of the six sides, we can then say that each side is equally
possible, in which case tossing a 6 is *not* equally possible with

tossing a non-6. Thus, tossing a non-6 is exclusively probable and no contradiction results.

The principle's applicability therefore depends upon exactly how the evidence is described. For example, if we are told that the evidence indicates indifferently that one of a die's six sides will be tossed, the principle decrees that each side is equipossible. The same result is generated if we are told that there is simply a report that one of the six sides will be tossed, or that there is simply a manufacturer's assurance of freedom from bias. On the other hand, the principle does not apply if we are merely told that the evidence indicates that one of the six sides will be tossed. Such evidence also indicates that one of 6 and non-6 will be tossed. And evidence that the die is biased also indicates that one of the six sides will be tossed. We must be told that the evidence is indifferent to each of the six sides or that there is no reason for preferring any of the six sides. Otherwise, the evidence-description does not fix the set of alternatives which is to carry the equal load.

The principle therefore does not try to create a knowledge of probabilities out of sheer ignorance.[6] It tries to generate probabilistic conclusions from information about limitations on the evidence in a given case, which is a sensible enterprise. Similarly, it avoids absurdly implying that, if we are only given that a proposition and its negation are each possible, the two are equally possible. The principle makes the two equipossible only on condition that the evidence indicates indifferently that one of the two is true. We must be told that much about the case.

Attending to the way evidence is described also accommodates reciprocal problem cases of the sort discussed by Keynes.[7] Imagine that x has a specific volume between 1 and 3 units but its precise volume is unknown. The volume's being between 1 and 2 is an alternative to its being between 2 and 3, and the two alternatives seem equipossible. Yet specific density is the reciprocal of specific volume, and therefore x's density is between 1 and $\frac{1}{3}$ unit. Since the precise density is also unknown, it seems that the alternative density ranges—1 to $\frac{2}{3}$ and $\frac{2}{3}$ to $\frac{1}{3}$—are also equipossible. But conjoining the two results implies that it both is and is not probable that x's volume falls between 1 and 2. Now, if the evidence in the case is indeed indifferent to equal volume ranges, the principle does dictate that 1 to 2 and 2 to 3 are equipossible. But then the evidence is not indifferent to equal density ranges.

Since it indicates that density is the reciprocal of volume, it must favour density ranges at one end, since it must treat the unequal ranges 1 to ½ and ½ to ⅓ indifferently. Hence the principle does not also imply that equal density ranges are equipossible.

The principle of indifference cannot tell the whole story about absolute probability, however. Applying the principle requires saying that the absolutely total evidence is probably indifferent. This involves appealing to prior evidence without using the principle itself. Otherwise an unacceptable regress would be started. Whether such a move can be defended will be examined in chapter 9. At the moment, we need only note that it is a separate move. It follows that the principle does not create an ideal-evidence paradox.[8] For example, we can confirm our estimate that evidence is probably indifferent to each side of a coin by tossing the coin a few times.

Indeed, indifference normally cannot tell even part of the story about absolute probability. To apply the principle, we need information that the absolutely total evidence contains no reason for preferring any alternative from a specified set. Usually our information indicates that subsequent evidence will not be impartial, e.g., that we shall see which side of the coin will be tossed. Only in rare circumstances, then, can the principle underwrite anything more than a relative claim. But such circumstances are possible in theory.

6. RATIONAL ACCEPTANCE

Understanding the concept of absolute probability can bring us closer to understanding an important epistemic dimension of knowledge. But anyone who denies probabilistic acceptance rules will likely find this connection doubtful. Something known is something that should be accepted, provided "should" expresses rational appraisal. If we cannot say the same for probability, how can claiming probability bring us closer to claiming knowledge?

Probabilistic acceptance rules often *are* suspect in the case of relative probability.[9] Something can be probable relative to given evidence when there is a good chance that new evidence will reverse the result. We should then wait for the new evidence before deciding. Similarly, an established scientific theory can be highly probable relative to received opinion when a scientist should not accept it because his investigations may well force a revision.

Sometimes, however, relative probability is all we can have, and in that case we should abide by it. For instance, even if we are all to die before a greyhound race finishes, we might still want to predict the winner correctly, merely for the sake of getting things right. In that event we should accept the probable winner, even though the probability is just relative.

We should accept something absolutely probable, provided we are justified in claiming that it is absolutely probable. We can then justifiably predict that further inquiry will not have an adverse effect. The degree of acceptance should be a function both of the degree of probability *and* of the degree of justification, however. For example, even if it is highly probable that energy sources will become increasingly scarce, we should not become firmly attached to the proposition if our justification for making the probability claim is not very strong.

Yet some will reject even cautious probabilistic acceptance rules in order to preserve consistency. According to an acceptance rule, if a conjunction of individually probable propositions is itself improbable, we should accept each conjunct while rejecting the conjunction, which is inconsistent. Those who dislike inconsistency therefore advocate a withholding policy, where what is to be withheld will depend upon the particular circumstances.[10]

A withholding policy does make sense when we can wait for further evidence to alter the situation. For example, we can say that one ticket in a fair lottery will win, and refuse to say of any ticket that it will lose, even though its losing is highly probable. We can wait until the winner is declared before accepting anything else. But if there are no prospects of improving the evidence, we should accept what is probable and any resulting inconsistencies. For instance, there is no foreseeable way to avoid conceding that probably one of my individually probable beliefs is false. I should therefore continue to accept each belief and yet, inconsistently, also accept the fallibilistic concession. Granted, I should not accept an internally inconsistent proposition. But that simply means that I should not accept "All my beliefs are true and yet one is false." It does not mean that I should not accept my several beliefs while rejecting their conjunction. And the closure rule "Accept anything entailed by accepted propositions" does not have enough independent strength to establish otherwise.[11]

We must remember that the ultimate aim here is to discover the truth of given propositions, not merely to avoid error. The avoidance of error can be realized by a program of minimal acceptance; knowledge cannot. Moreover, attaining knowledge involves more than accepting true propositions, since the latter can be achieved by a program of indiscriminate acceptance. The acceptance must also be authoritative, which rules out accepting just anything. The only way we can acquire such authority is to be governed by probability. Although this does mean that sometimes favoured propositions will be false, the cost is tolerable. More precisely, the cost is tolerable *if* the ultimate end is knowledge.

Granted, it might be possible to align knowledge with a maximum degree of probability and then adopt a policy that reconciles the pursuit of knowledge with the rejection of most probabilistic acceptance rules. For example, we might on this account claim knowledge that one lottery ticket will win and refuse to accept "Ticket *a* will lose," "Ticket *b* will lose," etc., because the degree of probability is not high enough in the latter cases. But such a program prevents us from seeking an authority that approximates the authority involved in knowledge when the latter is unattainable. Moreover, we must then accept anything that has maximum probability, while refusing to accept anything with less than the maximum, merely because we otherwise risk inconsistency. Viewed in itself, the differential treatment looks arbitrary; and the ground seems too weak to remove the arbitrariness. Consequently, a less restricted probabilistic rule seems the better course.

7. SUMMARY

Relative probability fails to capture an important dimension of knowledge because it is exclusively a function of someone's total evidence. Absolutely probability begins to close this gap, since it is partly a function of the absolutely total evidence. Certainty closes the gap completely and can now be explained as the limiting case of absolute probability.

CHAPTER THREE

Certainty

1. BEING SURE

Let us reserve "certain" for impersonal contexts and use "sure" for personal ascriptions. Thus, we shall say "It is certain" and "He is sure," but not "He is certain." Also, let us restrict "sure" to cases where someone finds something absolutely certain in a sense to be defined in the next section. Being sure does incorporate an absolute, but not one that qualifies a feeling. The absolute concerns what is found to be the case by the person who is sure.

Being sure is not intended to be a sophisticated state. A child can be sure that $2 + 2 = 4$ provided he can reckon that $2 + 2$ must equal 4. He need not be able to use the word "certain," and he need not know what the correct analysis of the concept is. He need merely appreciate the difference between holding that something is the case and holding that it must be the case.

Being sure is dispositional, in the sense that someone can be sure of something even though nothing actually occurs to him at the time. We can say that he is sure provided he would have responded to specific stimuli in suitable ways. This does not mean that being sure consists in a set of conditional responses. But it does mean that in order to make good the claim that someone is sure of something we need merely establish that he would have responded had the conditions been satisfied. For example, someone can on these grounds be said to be sure of something even when he is sound asleep.

Conviction is not sufficient for being sure, since someone can be convinced of God's existence without finding His existence certain. Conversely, it is possible to be sure of something without being convinced of it. For instance, a wife can find it certain that she has locked the door, hence be sure of it, and yet not be convinced of it because her husband expresses doubt. She has no reason for crediting her husband's attitude. Yet her feelings do waver in spite of her lack of reasons.

Cases are also possible in which someone fails to find something certain because his feelings interfere with his judgment. For example, an examinee can fail to be sure that an answer is correct solely because of a nervous reaction. Now, we can, and should, construct a concept of being sure according to which no one can fail to be sure of anything merely because of nonrational factors. We can construct such a concept by saying that, in a technical sense, someone is sure of something if, and only if, either he is sure of it in an ordinary sense or he would have been sure of it if, *ceteris paribus,* he had been controlled solely by rational considerations. Thus, the unconfident examinee is technically sure of the answer provided he would have been sure of it had he not been overcome by nerves.

Stretching the ordinary concept of being sure in this way does not empty the concept of meaning. No one who is unsure of something in an ordinary sense can be technically sure of it if his doubt stems from reasons and not irrational causes. For instance, someone who for philosophical reasons doubts the existence of external objects is not technically sure that he has a human body. He would be technically sure only if his doubt resulted from something like a phobia.

The point of stretching the concept is to keep it more in line with the concept of an ideal form of knowledge. Such an ideal makes no demands on our irrational nature. Realizing the ideal depends solely on our attitudes insofar as we are governed by rational considerations. Consequently, we need a concept of being sure that is compatible with irrational doubt.

2. ABSOLUTE CERTAINTY

We can define absolute certainty as the limiting case of absolute probability. Something is *absolutely certain,* given someone's total evidence at a given time, if, and only if, (i) it is plausible given that evidence, and (ii) there is no good counterevidence in relation to that evidence.

Although certainty in this sense is called absolute, it is still partly a function of someone's total evidence at a given time. The plausibility requirement is satisfied only if someone either has plausibility-conferring evidence or has a correct intuition. As a result, absolute certainty is not so absolute that nothing can be certain at one time and not at another, or that nothing can be certain in relation to one person's evidence and not in relation to another's. For example, it was not certain in 1800 that men would fly in planes in 1950, whereas it is certain now. Similarly, there may be regions of the world today where it is not certain that men have travelled to the moon because no one in those regions has evidence that makes such a thing plausible.

The point of attaching "absolute" to certainty is in part to emphasize that the absence of good counterevidence is a condition on the absolutely total evidence. The fact that someone possesses no good counterevidence at a given time is not enough to make something certain. He must *never* have such evidence, nor must anyone else. Again, some will worry about whether we can ever be justified in claiming that this condition is satisfied; but that worry will be considered in chapter 9.

This means that if something is certain given someone's evidence at a given time, it must remain certain given that same (or equivalent) evidence, regardless of how the evidence is augmented. Since certainty requires the absence of good counterevidence in the remaining evidence, merely adding further evidence cannot change anything. In this sense absolute certainty is a permanent condition.

Certainty is also absolute in virtue of incorporating a limit. We sometimes tend to think of certainty as resulting from the accumulation of enough positive evidence, in which case it is hard to see how the process could ever be completed. More support always seems possible, at least in principle. But a cumulative model of certainty is both unfortunate and unnecessary. We should think of it instead as resulting from the discreditation of counterevidence. We can understand how there can be *no* good counterevidence, whereas we cannot understand how there can be enough positive evidence. Being certain is like winning an election by shutting out the opposition—even if only one ballot is favourable and millions are against, if the negative ones are all spoiled, the official vote is 1 to 0 and the victory is still absolute. Certainty is not a matter of getting an indefinitely large number of supporting votes. It is a matter of getting at least one supporting vote and no opposing ones. Nothing can be more certain than this, in which case certainty does embody a coherent limit.

3. TRUTH

We shall so use "certain" that something certain need not be true. This may be contrary to ordinary usage, since "It is certain that p, and it is false that p" may be self-contradictory. On the other hand, the conjunction may only be self-defeating, as in the case of "I believe that p, and it is false that p." Indeed, the fact that "It is certainly true that p" is not clearly redundant might suggest that certainty in a plain sense can be independent of truth. In any case, even if there is no sanction in ordinary usage, there are three reasons for deciding to use "certain" in an independent way.

First, the decision preserves a continuity between certainty and absolute probability. In other words, certainty remains the limiting case of absolute probability. Second, by separating certainty from truth and then attaching both conditions to knowledge we give the sceptic two targets to shoot at, targets that would eventually have to be separated in any event. Third, as we shall eventually see, it is important to preserve a sharp distinction between claims about truth and claims about evidence. By formulating certainty exclusively in terms of plausibility and the absence of good counterevidence, and not adding a truth requirement, we can keep this distinction firmly before us.

Since certainty does not involve truth, certainty is distinct from any form of incorrigibility that requires a belief's truth as a condition of the belief's being held. Something certain can be believed without being true. Granted, there cannot be any way for someone to find out that a belief that is certain is really false, since finding this out would require the existence of good counterevidence and hence eliminate the certainty. But this simply means that we cannot coherently *say* that something is both certain and false. It does not mean that nothing can *be* both certain and false.

4. NECESSITY

Although there is an important connection between certainty and necessity, there are also important disconnections. Suppose that I say "It is certain that Thunder Bay is in Ontario." The certainty claim is successful only if I can defend the claim "It must be the case that Thunder Bay is in Ontario," i.e., only if I can avoid having to concede that Thunder Bay may not be in Ontario. Moreover, if I can make good the necessity claim, I thereby also make good the certainty claim. Thus, a certainty claim is justified if, and only if, the corresponding necessity claim is also justified. This is why a sceptic can challenge a certainty claim by challenging the necessity claim; e.g., he can challenge 'It is certain that there are external objects' simply by establishing that there may not be any.

This does not mean, however, that something certain must be necessary. Certainty in the present sense is independent of truth, whereas necessity is not. Thus, something certain can fail to be necessary because it is false. We cannot *say* that something certain fails to be necessary for this reason, of course, since we cannot justifiably say that something is both certain and false. But the theoretical possibility remains.

Moreover, unlike certainty, necessity is not temporal. We can say "It is now certain that men can travel in space, but it wasn't certain in 1800," whereas we cannot say the same thing using "necessary" in place of "certain." Unlike a certainty claim, a necessity claim is not about evidence. Nevertheless, a necessity claim is correct if the corresponding certainty claim can be correctly made about the evidence possessed by the person who makes the necessity claim. If "It is now certain, given my evidence, that men can travel in space" is correct, then so is "It must be the case that men can travel in space."

The necessity to which certainty can be linked is not logical necessity *if* logical necessity excludes the possibility of things having been otherwise. Although it must be the case that I exist, given that it is certain that I exist, it is possible for me not to have existed. Thus, although my existing is in a sense necessary, the necessity is not logical. Conversely, something logically necessary can fail to be certain; e.g., although "God exists" is uncertain, it can still be a logically necessary truth. Following Moore, let us say that whereas certainty correlates with *epistemic* necessity, certainty fails to correlate with logical necessity.

Epistemic necessity is also distinct from causal or nomic necessity. The epistemic necessity of my existence is not a matter of my existence being a necessary result of prior conditions. It is a function of the kind of evidence that bears on the question of whether I exist. Moreover, unlike epistemic necessity, nomic necessity does have counterfactual implications. For example, suppose that it is nomically necessary that human beings need oxygen to survive. It is therefore not only necessary that my living wife now has oxygen, but it is also necessary that she would have had oxygen had she been living in different circumstances. Granted, there may be the following connection between epistemic and nomic necessity: If an *A* instance nomically necessitates a B instance, the epistemic necessity of an A instance requires the epistemic necessity of a B instance; e.g., perhaps "The spark caused the explosion" is sound only if "If it is certain that a spark occurred in those circumstances, it is certain that an explosion followed" is also sound. But this does not mean that the nomic necessity is itself a case of epistemic necessity. A spark can cause an explosion even when there is no good evidence of its having done so, in which case there is nothing epistemically necessary about the occurrence.

Aligning certainty just with epistemic necessity means that a sceptic who universally disclaims certainty need not on that account disclaim logical necessity. He may have to refuse to claim nomic necessity, on the ground that we can never justify conditional certainty claims. But he can still make logical claims, albeit uncertain ones. He simply has to make it clear that "2 + 2 may not equal 4" does not entail "It is logically possible for 2 + 2 not to have equalled 4." A statement of the form "Maybe not" expresses doubt. It makes an epistemic point, not a logical point.

5. JUSTIFICATION

Certainty is different from justification because certainty is partly a function of the absolutely total evidence, whereas, as we shall see in more detail in chapter 9, justification is concerned with the type of evidence that someone has and in particular with how reliable it is. Thus, someone can justifiably claim that the world is certainly flat, if his relevant evidence is of a reliable sort, and yet the certainty claim can be incorrect, because there is good additional evidence that the earth is not flat. Conversely, a native on a primitive island who watches a helicopter land and quickly take off can correctly claim that men certainly do fly in machines, even though his evidence is not yet reliable enough to justify such a claim.

Since certainty does not involve justification, it is distinct from certainty in Firth's *warrant-evaluating* sense. A warrant-evaluating certainty must have a maximum degree of warrant, where maximum warrant is "a property that statements possess in relation to . . . the 'warrant-conferring' characteristics of a particular person at a particular time." This tends to make maximum warrant exclusively a matter of what a person's evidence at a given time is like and not at all a matter of what the remaining evidence is like. Hence it falls short of describing conditions of certainty.[1]

Firth comes closer to the present notion when he introduces a *testability-evaluating* sense, which demands that the person in question cannot subsequently have reasonable doubts, however slight. But this can be taken to imply that something is a *testability-evaluating* certainty only if the given person cannot subsequently fail to be justified in claiming certainty, regardless of what new evidence is added. This condition is stronger than the present requirements on certainty. The present concept does demand that any new counterevidence *is* discredited by further evidence. But it does not require the given person to *have* such discrediting evidence. Thus, the native who sees a helicopter for the first time might subsequently be confronted by forceful peer objections that he cannot answer, although they could be answered by us. The proposition "Men fly in machines" then fails to be a testability-evaluating certainty given his evidence because he does subsequently *have* reasonable doubts. But the proposition is certain in the present sense, given his evidence, because his doubts could have been removed by evidence that he does not possess.

Since certainty is distinct from justification, the word "certain" is not being used here in the normative sense described by Quinton when he says: "There is a normative element about the word, it asserts that the statements it is applied to do not *need* any further justification, that it is *right* to act on them with complete confidence, that it would be *irrational* to doubt them."[2] The present use of "certain" *is* normative to the extent that calling a proposition "certain" does involve an assessment of someone's evidence. It makes a claim about how his evidence bears on the proposition and also about how the remaining evidence so bears. But the present use is not normative to the extent that it does not pronounce on whether his evidence justifies such an assessment. The proposition "Men fly in machines" can be certain given what the native sees, and yet he might need further evidence before he can be justified in accepting it, or before he has a right to act on it with complete confidence, or before it would no longer be irrational for him to doubt it. The normative considerations connected with justification are thus distinct from those connected with certainty.

6. INDUBITABILITY

If indubitability consists simply in the complete absence of good counterevidence, certainty does involve indubitability. Something is certain only if there is absolutely no good ground for doubting it, regardless of who might possess such a ground or when it is possessed.

Unfortunately, this requirement is sometimes confused with the condition that something is certain only if it is *impossible* for there to be a good ground for doubting it. It is true that certainty cannot be combined with the existence of good counterevidence—i.e., that such a *combination* is impossible. But it is not true that the impossibility of good counterevidence is itself a condition of certainty. This step from a nonmodal to a modal condition is not a part of the concept of certainty. If the step is legitimate, its legitimacy must be established by argument. As we shall see in chapter 8, a major source of scepticism resides in the assumption that certainty requires the impossibility of good counterevidence and not merely the absence of such evidence. Consequently, it is important to be clear that a step is involved and that the step needs defending.

7. PRACTICE AND THEORY

Notions of good counterevidence, epistemic necessity, and certainty can be relativized to practical purposes. For example, if a train is scheduled to arrive at 9:05 A.M. and it almost always runs on time, we can for most practical purposes correctly say "The train is certain to be here at 9:05 A.M." For most purposes the occasional tardiness is not a good ground for doubt. But if we are in a life-or-death situation and have to decide whether to wait for the train or drive for help, the tardiness can for that purpose be a good reason for doubt.[3]

Even when certainty-governing standards are tightened as the stakes increase, these standards are still relative to practical purposes. Imagine that the train has never run late and that there is no other customary reason for thinking it will be late, even given that our purposes are life-or-death. Then imagine that a philosopher tries to raise doubts on the ground that everything may just be a dream. His ground can be dismissed as irrelevant, since our purpose presupposes that a life is in danger and hence that we are not dreaming. The point is not that the philosopher's argument for doubt is poor but that it is irrelevant. Once the question "What is the evidence like for predicting the train's arrival?" is linked to the purpose of saving a life, this automatically excludes the possibility that we are all in a dream.

Standards can also be relativized to disciplinary commitments. For example, an historian cannot as such cite the general fallibility of human memory as a ground for doubting that a world war began in 1914. If such a ground worked, everything he tried to do as an historian would become doubtful. Consequently, within the discipline of history, proposing such a ground is to propose inadmissible evidence. An historian cannot treat it seriously and still purport to be doing history.

For our present philosophical purposes, however, no proposed ground for doubt can be ruled inadmissible, either by virtue of the purposes at hand or in light of our disciplinary commitments. Our objective is solely the discovery of truth, which means that the standard that governs what counts as good evidence in this context is absolute. Moreover, there is no antecedent commitment to a specific kind of conclusion, since on principle anything is vulnerable to legitimate challenge.

Contrary to what Peirce suggests, that does not mean that we are flirting with merely idle doubts.[4] Granted, philosophical doubt applies equally to different practical options; e.g., it makes both "The train will arrive on time" and its negation doubtful. And we cannot take practical steps to remove it. But it can be used as a weapon against dogmatism, even in the practical sphere. Moreover, it can make a profound difference to our intellectual life. We must remember that the search for truth is an independent activity, that it is not subordinate to further ends. Consequently, doubt that makes no difference in practical affairs can still have a substantial impact in the theoretical arena. Furthermore, theoretical arguments can be constructed to remove it.[5]

8. SUMMARY

Certainty is absolute in three respects. First, it is partly a function of the absolutely total evidence. Second, it involves the complete absence of good counterevidence and to this extent constitutes the limit of a series. Third, it incorporates standards of evidence that are not relative to any practical purposes or restricted by prior disciplinary commitments.

Certainty is distinct from being sure on the one hand and truth on the other. Moreover, certainty is not to be confused with justification. Certainty can therefore be an independent condition of knowledge. Before considering the analysis of knowledge, however, let us first take a closer look at truth.

CHAPTER 4

Truth

1. ABSOLUTE TRUTH

We have made certainty absolute in the qualified sense that something certain at one time must be certain at any other time *if* the same plausibility condition is satisfied. We shall make truth absolute in the unqualified sense that something true at one time must be true at any other time.

Adopting an absolute conception of truth incorporates a decision about how to identify truth bearers. For example, suppose that an object changes from red to green and someone says of the object "It is red" both before and after the change. There is a sense in which he says the same thing on both occasions, in which case the same thing is true on one occasion, false on another. But there is also a sense in which he says something different, because he refers to the object at different stages in its history. Similarly, if two people say "It is red" of different objects at the same time, they in a sense say the same thing, and yet in another sense they say something different because the objects referred to are different. Given that we so identify truth bearers that different truth bearers are involved in each of the above cases, truth is absolute.

Thus, if we say "It was once true that John could eat hot peppers, but it's no longer true," we shall understand this to imply that his being able to eat peppers *then* was the case and his being able to eat peppers *now* is not the case. His having the first temporalized ability is still the case now and his having the second ability was not the case even then. To this extent nothing has changed its truth value.

This means that grammatically different sentences can be used to state the same truth; e.g., "John is able to eat peppers," used then, and "John was able to eat peppers," used now, state the same truth. Indeed, if we want to put sentences on a par with other truth bearers, we shall have to say that the two sentences are the same, or that they are different tokens of the same sentence type, just as we shall have to say that they express the same proposition or belief. Similarly, we must be able to describe the same truth by using different constructions, such as "It was true in 1800 that men would fly" and "It is now true that men have flown." Moreover, we must so use "what was asserted" and "what is the case" that what was asserted in 1800 by "Men will fly" is now the case because men have flown. Given such adjustments, we can preserve an absolute view of truth.

Since truth is absolute, it is objective, in the sense that something true need not be believed (or accepted, supposed, considered, etc.), and also in the sense that something believed need not be true, regardless of who believes it or how many believe it. Psychological considerations are completely independent of truth values. Otherwise truth values could change with a change in psychological responses.

Making truth absolute also separates it from epistemic conditions, such as plausibility, certainty, or justification. Thus, the following conjunctions are logically consistent.

> It is true that p; it is not plausible, probable, or certain that p; nor is there any justification for believing that p.

> It is certain that p and one is justified in believing that p; it is false that p.

Granted, both conjunctions are odd, since the first one is correct only if its first conjunct lacks plausibility, and the second one is correct only if its second conjunct is unjustified. But this does not make the conjunctions self-contradictory, any more than the oddness of "It is true that p; I do not believe that p" discloses a contradiction in a truth's not being believed by me.

Granted too, ordinary English does not always mark a distinction between truth-value considerations and epistemic considerations. We commonly use "That's true" to mean "That's justified." The present use of "true" is to that extent distinctive. But it is not on that account incoherent. Of course, some will feel that if we do separate truth in order to make it absolute, we shall put truth beyond our grasp. Yet there is nothing obvious about such a result, and I shall argue in chapter 13 that it does not in fact follow. Indeed, the fact that the objection is provoked by the separation is a good reason for performing it, since requiring truth of knowledge then helps to make knowledge claims that much more interesting.

2. TRUTH AND REALITY

Truth is a function of reality to the extent, e.g., that a statement is true if, and only if, what it states really is the case. This is so regardless of whether the statement is negative, conditional, subjective, or logically necessary. The statement "3 is necessarily greater than 1" is true insofar as what it states really is the case, since it really is the case that 3 is necessarily greater than 1.

This means that reality must be unchangeable in a way corresponding to the absolute nature of truth. Although individuals can change, their being what they are at a given time cannot change. For example, although my son has changed from short to tall, his having been short in 1968 has not changed. To this extent reality is just as absolute as truth.

There is an intimate connection between what the claim that a statement is true asserts and what its object statement asserts. There are analogously close connections between what is asserted by truth claims about beliefs, propositions, sentences, and suppositions, and what is believed, proposed, said, or supposed in each instance. Now, some would go so far as to say that a truth claim asserts what its object statement asserts, that, although the two differ in other respects, their assertive content is the same. Thus, Strawson suggests that we can always paraphrase the truth claim "p is true" by using a construction like "As p says, p." According to this view, we thereby concede that the truth claim is about the statement p while preserving the assertive identity of the claim and statement. Such a view is often called a *redundancy theory*.[1]

Although the redundancy theory draws attention to three important features of truth, it oversteps its support. First, although "p is true" asserts *that* what p states to be the case actually is the case, it does not assert *that which* p states to be the case. Even Strawson is willing to paraphrase an unspecific truth claim like "What the Pope said is true" as "It is as the Pope said." If this type of analysis is then applied to the specific "The Pope's statement, that war is futile, is true," the proper paraphrase is "It is as the Pope's statement, that war is futile, says," which is different from the redundant "As the Pope says, war is futile."

Second, we should be careful about regarding truth as a property, or "is true" as a predicate. A predicative view can easily obscure the fact that a truth claim asserts that what its object statement states actually is the case. But we can leave proper room for this connection without adopting a redundancy theory. Indeed, if we are careful, we can even go so far as to say that "*p* is true" predicates of *p* the-being-the-case-of-what . . . states.

Third, the word "true" can be effectively eliminated by paraphrasing, but without being committed to assertive redundancy. For instance, we can adopt the truth formula introduced by Prior and developed in detail by Williams, according to which "*p* is true" is roughly formalized as "For some *x,* both *p* states that *x,* and *x.*"[2] Modifications can then be added to cover cases where "*p*" is a definite description (e.g., "What the Pope said"), or where *p* is a proposition, or where *p* is a sentence, or where the truth claim presupposes that *p* states that *x.* Granted, some will worry that using a quantifier commits us to entities and that in this case the entities are bizarre. But the commitment is only to saying that there is something stated by a given statement, not to saying that that something is an entity. Others will be concerned that verifying the quantified assertion in a particular instance requires reporting what *p* states in the first conjunct and asserting what *p* states in the second, as in "This states that snow is white, and snow is white." But this simply means that the propositional function "For some *x,* . . . states that *x,* and *x*" does not incorporate a predicate of *p* in any familiar sense, which is hardly a distressing result.

Grover, Camp, and Belnap develop something akin to a redundancy theory by taking a truth sentence to be related to its alleged object sentence in roughly the way pronouns are related to their nominal antecedents.[3] An unspecific truth sentence like "That's true" is then held to be a *prosentence.* It differs syntactically and pragmatically from its original, but not semantically. On the other hand, a specific truth sentence like "'Snow is white' is true" is held to be the conjunction "Snow is white; that's true," where the second conjunct is a prosentence. This means that the truth sentence does not actually refer to the sentence it seems to be about. The prosentential theory welcomes such a result on the ground that referential truth sentences are committed to special entities like statements. But again, although a referential "*p* is true" is committed to saying that there is a statement that is true, this is not a commitment to regarding such a statement as an entity. For example, we need not assign both a numerical and a qualitative identity to statements; nor need we locate them in a special world. Moving from "There is a statement, *p,* which is true" to "Statement *p* is an entity" is just as gratuitous as moving from

"There is a contradiction in his view" to "The contradiction in his view is an entity." Consequently, there is no reason to avoid making truth sentences referential, in which case there is no reason to favour a prosentential theory.

3. PARADOX

Can an absolute conception of truth avoid admitting statements which have opposing truth values? For example, if

(1) Statement (1) is false

is a statement, what (1) states actually is the case if, and only if, (1) is false. Thus, according to the absolute view, (1) is true if, and only if, (1) is false, which means that if (1) is either true or false, it is both.

The simple reply that (1) is neither true nor false affords no real escape from this problem, since the same problem emerges if "false" is replaced by "not true." Indeed, for any proposed solution of the form "A statement need neither be true nor have a negative truth value at level n," the remark

(2) Statement (2) has a negative truth value at level $n + 1$

creates the same problem. Moreover such a solution is ad hoc unless it provides an independent explanation of why the given remarks lack truth value.[4]

A flat denial that sentence (1) embodies a statement is also unsatisfactory, since sentence (1) does contain meaningful words, is syntactically respectable, and can be linked in a quasilogical way with remarks like "(1) is a statement." Now, Grover tries to offer a rationale for holding that sentence (1) lacks content.[5] She invokes the prosentential theory of truth and claims that (1) is a prosentence that lacks an original and hence has no content. But as we have seen, the prosentential theory is unconvincing, and the implication that (1) lacks content merely exaggerates the problem. Something must be done to overcome the initial impression that (1) has meaning before such a result can count in the theory's favour.

Denying (1)'s legitimacy merely on the ground that it is self-referring is equally ineffective. The self-referential sentence

(3) Sentence (3) is in English

is legitimate, and it is hard to see why self-reference should be singled out as a culprit in the case of (1). Also, if a hierarchical order is imposed in the case of "true" and "false," we cannot make unrestricted claims like "Every statement is either true or not true," which would be a significant loss. Moreover, the question of independent motivation still persists. And "true" then has to mean something like "true in nothing higher than the object language."[6]

Can anything be done to undermine the legitimacy of sentences like (1), i.e., to establish that they cannot be used to make statements that have opposing truth values? If not, then perhaps we should rethink our decision to employ a concept of absolute truth that resists a redundancy theory. Indeed, perhaps we should accept the prosential theorist's suggestion that the problem sentences are really just contentless prosentences and dismiss any contrary intuition as mistaken. Before doing so, however, we should first look more carefully at the referential character that the problem sentences must have if truth claims do refer to object statements or the like. If a solution can be found along such lines, it will help both to confirm a referential analysis and to protect an absolute conception from generating contradictions.

4. REFERENCE AND DEGENERACY

Imagine that London is suddenly destroyed by a nuclear explosion but that John does not know this and says "London is on the Thames." There is a sense in which nothing exists to which he refers when he uses "London." His reference is to this extent a failure. Nevertheless, there is also a sense in which there *is* something to which he refers when he uses "London," just as there is something to which his more knowledgeable wife refers when she says "London does not exist, it was destroyed in an explosion." To this extent his reference does not break down. Let us say that in using "London" in this context he fails to refer *extensionally,* although he succeeds in referring *intentionally*. Thus, when his wife uses "London" she succeeds in referring intentionally, but she does not even try to refer extensionally and hence confronts no failure.

Allowing intentional referents in cases of extensional failure does not imply that there are nonexistent entities. Intentional referents are not subject to the distinction between numerical and qualitative identity and hence are not entities. For instance, the city to which John intentionally refers and the city to which his wife intentionally refers are the same city. But it makes no sense to say of them either that they are qualitatively and numerically the same or that they are only qualitatively the same. The division simply has no application in this case, which means that we are not dealing with entities of any sort, nonexistent or otherwise.

A purported intentional reference succeeds if there is something to which the name intentionally refers. A purported extensional reference succeeds if the name intentionally refers to something that does really exist. Further distinctions of this sort are possible. For example, a *fictional* reference succeeds if a name intentionally refers to something that is fictional; a *dream* reference succeeds if a name intentionally refers to something in a dream. Not every instance of referring lends itself to such a distinction, however. If we refer to a property or a species, a successful intentional reference is all we can get. If we intentionally refer to the property $\varnothing$ and there is a property $\varnothing$ to which we refer, we cannot then sensibly ask whether the property $\varnothing$ also exists, or has being, or is a fictional thing, or occurs in a dream. The question of successful reference in this case ends with the question of successful intentional reference. Thus, allowing properties as intentional referents does not invite questions like "Is a property numerically different from the individual who has it?" or "Do properties exist in space?" It does not transform properties into entities. The same point holds for references to statement types or to belief types.

An extensional reference breaks down if nothing really exists to which we intentionally refer. An intentional reference breaks down if there is nothing to which we refer. For example, imagine that someone says "It is round." Normally "it" acquires an intentional reference contextually, because of some other referential activity in the situation; e.g., the speaker nods his head, or points, or looks straight at a prominent object, or earlier asks "What shape is the table?" or subsequently says "The table's shape is deceptive." In this sense the pronoun's reference is *parasitical*. Imagine that the speaker is hallucinating and that no table really exists. In that case his use of "it" fails to refer extensionally, although it has a successful intentional reference. But now imagine that there is absolutely nothing in the context from which "it" can derive an intentional reference: no gesture, no antecedent or subsequent referring noun. In that case there is nothing to which "it" refers, and the pronoun fails to have an intentional reference. There is a complete referential collapse. Let us say that "it" is then an *empty* parasite.

Sentences containing empty parasites can still be said to have meaning. If your use of "it" in "It is round" is empty and mine is not, we do in a sense mean the same thing by what we say. Our remarks differ only referentially. Granted, in ordinary discourse the line between meaning and reference is not always drawn so sharply. We could in some plain sense say that your use of "It is round" is meaningless or that it means something different from mine. But there also seems a sense in which we do mean the same thing, even though what we say is referentially quite different. And it is useful to use "mean" in this second way here.

We have seen that truth is absolute only if we make the identification of a truth bearer sensitive to reference. If an object changes from round to square, the remark "It is round" remains true only if the remark is identified as something that refers to the given object at a given time. The remark is therefore different from any subsequent "It is round" that refers to the object at a later time. Now, if the identification of truth bearers must be sensitive to reference, a sentence containing an empty parasite cannot be a truth bearer at all. If the sentence "It is round" contains an empty "it," there is no way to identify what the sentence is being used to refer to, in which case there is no truth-bearing statement, remark, or belief to pick out. Although the sentence is meaningful, and although in a meaning-sensitive sense it *is* used to say something, it is not used to make a statement in the relevant reference-sensitive sense.

Call a sentence that suffers a complete referential collapse *degenerate*. A degenerate sentence is therefore not used to make a statement and it cannot be said to have a truth value, including negative truth values. If "It is round" is degenerate, so is any negative operation, such as "It is not round" or "It is not the case that it is round." The emptiness of "it" infects all such operations. Consequently, we cannot say that the sentence is false, or not true, or characterized by a true denial at some level. An empty "It is round" fails to be true in the way a command fails to be true, not in the way "Macbeth was ambitious" fails to be true when it purportedly refers extensionally to Macbeth. Whereas we can point out that Macbeth was not a real person, we cannot say that "it" does not really exist.

Empty parasites are not the only sources of degeneracy. For example, imagine that someone says "A representative theory of perception rules out knowledge of an external world" and in confusion uses "representative theory of perception" to embrace two distinct, albeit similar, theories. The remark is not ambiguous, in the sense that it does not refer to just one of the two theories in a way that makes it hard to tell which. Nor is it vague, in the sense that it does not refer to a general theory of which each theory is a species. Instead, it wrongly confuses the two theories and, in the mistaken belief that there is only one, purportedly refers to "that" theory. As a result, the remark fails to refer to anything intentionally and the sentence is degenerate. The sentence with its given meaning therefore lacks truth value, although if one of the two theories does exclude external-world knowledge, the comment can lead to an important truth.

5. AVOIDING PARADOX

We can use the notion of degeneracy to preserve the coherence of the absolute conception of truth and a referential view of truth claims.

Sentence (1) is degenerate. It purportedly refers to the statement made by using sentence (1). In so doing it by implication purportedly refers to what (1) is being used to say. But the expression "what (1) is used to say" is a parasite. It has to get its reference from some other feature of the situation. Yet there is no such feature in this case. The only possible answer we can give to "To what are you referring when you refer to what (1) says?" is "that statement (1) is false," which involves the very reference in question. Consequently, the parasitical reference is empty and (1) is degenerate. This means that (1) has no truth value at all and therefore cannot have opposing values.

Altering (1) to a sentence about a sentence, as in

(5) Sentence (5) is false

does not change anything. Although (5) does successfully refer to itself, it also by implication refers to what (5) is used to say—or, more strictly, to the negation of what (5) is used to say. This is still a necessarily empty reference. Hence (5) is degenerate.

Granted, degeneracy does not characterize

(6) Sentence (6) is degenerate,

since (6) simply refers to itself and to its own referential structure, which involves no parasitical reference. But since (6) is not degenerate, it is false and no paradox results from this. On the other hand, the sentence

(7) Sentence (7) is either false or degenerate

is degenerate, since (7) also implicitly and parasitically refers to what (7) says. Moreover, even though

(8) Sentence (7) is degenerate

is true, this does not make (7) itself true precisely because (7) is degenerate. Unlike (7), (8) simply refers to (7) and to (7)'s referential structure, which involves no empty parasites.

Degeneracy can be assigned to other familiar problem sentences, such as the pair

(9) Sentence (10) is true [and]
(10) Sentence (9) is false.

Sentence (9) purportedly refers to "what (10) says." Hence it implicitly refers to "what (9) says," then again to "what (10) says," and so on indefinitely. The references are parasitical and unavoidably empty, resulting in degeneracy. The pair is in this respect like

John said what Mary said [and]
Mary said what John said

where there is absolutely no independent indication of what either person said.

Degeneracy can also be used to explain the oddness of the positive counterparts of apparent contradictions. For example,

(11) Sentence (11) is true

is in no danger of having opposing truth values. But its having a truth value would be a curiosity, since it is true if, and only if, it is true, and false if, and only if, it is false. We can avoid such a result by noting that it too purportedly refers to "what (11) says" and hence is degenerate.

Classifying problem sentences as degenerate does not rule out all self-reference. But it does prohibit the self-ascription of truth values. This much in a Tarskian hierarchical theory, or in a Russellian type theory, is sound. Yet appealing to degeneracy tolerates a general claim like "Every statement is either true or false," even though the claim itself falls within its own domain. The claim refers to what is stated by any given statement, but this is not a parasitical reference. In other words, the claim's intentional reference need not be derived from any other reference in the context. In particular it need not be derived from a reference to what each statement within the claim's domain states. Hence no circularity is created and the reference is complete. The general claim is therefore unlike "The present statement is either true or false," which *is* degenerate.

Degenerate sentences are not meaningless, and hence the problem sentences need not be dismissed as meaningless. Their defect is referential, not one of content. We can therefore respect the fact that they are composed of meaningful words, are syntactically well formed, and can enter into quasilogical connections. On the other hand, we can say that the problem sentences fail to embody statements, or express beliefs, in reference-sensitive senses of such expressions. Thus we can retain the general principle "Every statement that has the type of identity required of a truth bearer must have a truth value." In other words, although there are truth gaps among declarative sentences, there are no gaps among statements of the sort to bear truth values.

Degeneracy can also be assigned to other sentences that do not contain truth predicates but which seem to have opposing truth values. For example,

(12) Heterologicality is heterological

seems to be equivalent to its own negation when "heterological" means "not a property of itself." But a sentence of the form "x is heterological" implicitly refers to a property that x lacks in virtue of which x is heterological. For instance, "Wisdom is heterological" implicitly refers to a property that wisdom lacks in virtue of which wisdom is not a self-property. Such a reference is parasitical and it can be nourished in this last instance by citing wisdom as the referent. But in the case of (12) the reference is necessarily empty. If in answer to "To what property are you referring?" we say "not being a self-property, i.e., heterologicality," we thereby implicitly refer to a property that heterologicality has in virtue of which it lacks the property of not being a self-property. And the only explanation of this reference we can offer is "heterologicality," which means that no independent explanation is available. Thus, (12) contains an empty parasite and is degenerate. (The same type of diagnosis holds for "Autologicality is autological," where "autological" means "a self-property.")

Russell's class-membership paradox can be similarly dissolved. The sentence

(13) The class of all classes that are not self-members is not a
      self-member

seems to be equivalent to its own negation. But a sentence of the
form "c is not a self-member" implicitly refers to that which c is
not in virtue of which c is not a self-member. We can explain such
a reference in the case of "The class of dogs is not a self-member"
by citing "a dog." But in the case of (13) all we can say is "a non-
self-membered class," which implicitly refers to that which the
class is in virtue of which it is self-membered. Thus no terminating explanation is available and the reference is empty, which
means that (13) is degenerate (as is its affirmative counterpart).
Hence (13) is not a genuine contradiction.

We should avoid transferring (13)'s defectiveness to the property of not being a self-membered class. Assigning the property to
a class does involve a parasitical reference. But the parasite is not
always empty. The predicate "is not a self-member" is not like the
predicate "is beside this" where "this" is an empty parasite. The
emptiness results from the way the predicate is used in (13), not
from the predicate's independent structure. Thus the class of all
non-self-membered classes is perfectly well defined and we can
retain the abstraction principle "A class is definable for each
legitimate predicate" in this case.

This means that the class of all non-self-membered classes
should not be assimilated to the barber who shaves all and only
non-self-shavers.[7] The barber is clearly impossible, since he
shaves himself if, and only if, he does not. Therefore, any preten-
der must be bearded or hairless or female or in some other way
fall outside the set by reference to which the barber is described.
But this is not a problematic result because there is nothing independently attractive about the possibility of the barber's existing.
The class of all non-self-membered classes, on the other hand,
does initially seem possible and we should do what we can to
respect this intuition.

Degeneracy probably won't remove all apparent paradoxes.
For example, suppose that a sentence is *groundless* if it has at
least one sentence in its domain that in turn has at least one
sentence in its domain, and so on indefinitely. Self-referring sentences are all groundless. Consider

(14) Grounded sentences do not generate liar paradoxes.[8]

If (14) is grounded, it falls within its own domain and hence is groundless. Yet if it is groundless by virtue of falling within its own domain, it is, it seems, grounded. Thus it seems that (14) is grounded if, and only if, it is not, and we have an apparent contradiction. I don't see that (14) is degenerate. But the fact—if it is a fact—that degeneracy cannot be used to eliminate paradox in this case does not bear adversely on the absolute conception of truth. The trouble starts with the apparent result that (14) is both grounded and groundless, not in the corollary that (14) is both true and false. Hence this contradiction should not be laid at the feet of a theory of truth. On the other hand, paradoxes that do seem to be generated specifically by an absolute view of truth *can* be dissolved by citing the degeneracy of the problem sentences. Hence the absolute view is logically innocent.

6. CORRESPONDENCE

A true statement must have a correspondent in the sense that what a true statement states must be a fact, in a broad sense that includes negative facts, conjunctive facts, subjunctive facts, and necessary facts. But to say this is not in itself to offer a distinctive *theory,* since even coherence theorists and pragmatists are prepared to concede as much. The question, then, is whether it confronts serious problems along the way. I doubt that it does have extra commitments and shall try to defend this view by comparing it with what might fairly be called "correspondence theories."

Correspondence theories generally treat the correspondents of true statements as entities. For example, Russell expressly says that "facts, . . . just as much as particular chairs and tables, are part of the real world."[9] As a result he is moved by parsimony to keep the variety of facts in the world minimal. Hamlyn views facts as constituting a separate metaphysical category: "The notion of a fact is a *categorial* notion; it picks out a distinct category of entities."[10] He concedes that a fact need not be "something in the world in a concrete sense," but he still thinks that a fact is an entity. Mackie goes farther than this when he says: "I do not see how we can deny that a particular aspect of reality is picked out by the sentence "The sun is hot," and that this quite objective feature is what we call a fact. . . . [The] sentence reports . . . something quite real and concrete, and the word "fact" merely enables us to talk generally about this sort of thing."[11] Chisholm takes things even farther when he holds that a *(de dicto)* belief is true only if a state of affairs obtains, that a state of affairs is itself an entity, and hence that a state of affairs that obtains is an existing entity.[12]

An absolute conception of truth contains no such view. Granted, something is true only if there is a fact in virtue of which it is true. Hence, given that some things are true, there are facts. This means that for some interpretation we can endorse formulae like

$$(p)(Tp \supset (\exists x)(x = fp)$$
$$(p)((\exists y)(y = tp) \supset (\exists x)(x = fp))$$

where "Tp" means "It is true that p," "fp" means "the fact that p," and "tp" means "the truth that p." Moreover, there might even be some point in saying that, on the one hand, there are things like tables and chairs and, on the other hand, there are facts. Hence we can even give qualified approval for

$$(\exists x)(\exists y)(Cx \cdot Fy)$$

where "C" means "is a chair" and "F" means "is a fact." But I don't see that concessions of this sort put facts in the real world, or create a special metaphysical category, or present facts as entities, concrete or otherwise.[13]

My reluctance to read a metaphysics into the concession that there are facts stems from the belief that adopting a metaphysical position requires doing something extra, something like assigning both a numerical and a qualitative identity to facts. We can sensibly talk of facts being the same or different, and we can spend a good deal of time investigating the conditions under which given facts are the same. But I don't think that we are authorized to say of two facts that they are qualitatively but not numerically the same. For example, the fact that the evening star is bright is the same as the fact that the morning star is bright because the two stars are the same. Yet it makes no clear sense to say that the two facts are both numerically and qualitatively the same. Thus, if x is not the evening star but is qualitatively the same as the evening star, it makes no clear sense to say that the fact that x is bright is qualitatively but not numerically the same as the fact that the evening star is bright. This is the point at which we both start to do metaphysics and yet go beyond the base provided by the absolute conception of truth. It may be that the farther step should be taken. But because it is a farther step, the absolute conception is not committed to it.

Similarly, adopting a metaphysical view of facts involves holding that they are the sort of thing of which we can ask the question "Are they temporally, or causally, or spatially related to physical objects?" Even if we deny that they enter into such relationships, as long as we treat them as the sort of thing of which we can sensibly ask such a question, we go farther than the simple view that there are facts. We start to invest them with a significant thinghood. We also go farther if, in holding that facts are a part of reality, we imply that, although unicorns are unreal, the fact that a unicorn is unihorned is real. And we take another step if we construe facts as the actual obtaining of eternal entities. Granted, it is a fact that dogs are affectionate only if there is a state of affairs—viz., dogs being affectionate—that actually obtains. But this does not mean that such a state of affairs is an entity, eternal or otherwise. Calling something an "entity" generally goes byond simply saying that there is such a thing.

Indeed, the absolute conception of truth is not merely uncommitted to construing facts as entities. It is actually hostile to such a view. Since it regards truth as completely objective, it allows the possible truth of "There are no (contingent) entities." This proposition could not possibly be true if facts were entities, since then the fact that there are no entities would itself have to be an entity, in which case there could be no such fact and hence no such truth. In this respect, the absolute conception does not merely avoid sharing the typical metaphysics of a correspondence theory. It actually opposes such a metaphysics.

Similar remarks apply to the absolute conception's attitude toward truth bearers. It concedes that there are such bearers but declines to regard them as entities. Indeed, in preserving the possible truth of "There are no entities," it implies that they are not entities. As a result, unlike some correspondence theories, the absolute conception need not worry about the things to which it assigns truth. For example, we can say that a proposition—in a technical what-is-believed (said, stated, etc.) sense—is true without in any way implying that the proposition is an entity.

7. SUMMARY

Making truth absolute preserves a close link between truth and reality. Indeed, the link is so close that truth claims about statements are in a sense assertive operations on what their object statements state. But they are not on that account simply reaffirmations of alleged object statements. They do retain a distinctive assertive role.

An absolute view of truth does not generate contradictions. The apparently contradictory sentences are all degenerate and hence cannot be used to make statements in a relevant sense. Moreover, an absolute view is not committed to the metaphysics that is often associated with a correspondence theory. If anything, it is opposed to such a commitment. Thus, attaching absolute truth to knowledge neither involves us in contradiction nor underwrites a contentious metaphysics.

CHAPTER FIVE

Knowledge

1. KNOWLEDGE AS AN IDEAL

The knowledge of truth represents an ideal that we generally all seek to attain. The higher the ideal, the more interesting the attainability question becomes. Thus, the present task is to outline an ideal that is as high as possible, but compatible with not being patently unrealistic.

Although some link with ordinary usage should be preserved—since the ideal initially takes shape in ordinary thought—there is no need to remain entirely faithful to a preconceived sense. We can try to describe an ideal that goes beyond anything envisaged in ordinary contexts, prior to debating whether the goal can be realized.

An ideal form of knowledge must satisfy at least four conditions:

(i) The knower must be sure of what he knows.
(ii) What is known must be absolutely certain.
(iii) The knower must be permanently justified in being sure.
(iv) Any proposition must be true if the *(ceteris paribus)* knowledge of its negation would have destroyed the knower's justification for being sure.

Each condition will attract sceptical objections, but none is obviously unsatisfiable. Of course, there may be others. For example, some might think that an emotional element should be included and that the first condition fails to reflect this need. But it is a hard condition to articulate. In any case, it probably would not be a separate focus of sceptical concern. Consequently, for the purpose of challenging the sceptic, we can regard these four conditions as jointly sufficient.

2. BEING SURE

The expression "being sure" should be understood in the technical sense defined in chapter 3, section 2, to include cases where someone is not sure in an ordinary sense but would have been sure had he responded from rational motives.

The reason for requiring sureness is that knowledge is to embody a personal ideal, which means that it must involve a subjective response. We are not interested in the impersonal type of knowledge that can be contained in a memo or a library, although the concept of impersonal knowledge might be regarded as an extension of the present concept.

The reason for requiring technical sureness is that knowledge concerns our attitudes insofar as we are governed by reason. Knowledge makes demands on our rational judgment, not on our feelings. Now, some may prefer to adopt a more ambitious ideal, one that requires a knower to be sure in an ordinary sense. But I doubt that anything is to be gained by such a change. I doubt that any sceptic would argue that the addition makes a crucial difference. Moreover, describing the ideal in terms of technical sureness reflects our ordinary use of "know." For example, we say that a self-deceiver knows something that he refuses to accept. He is not in an ordinary sense sure of what he knows, but he is technically sure of it.

The counterfactual component of technical sureness is apt to create misunderstanding. It merely implies that, other things being equal, someone would have been sure had he responded rationally. It does not imply that he would have been sure regardless of what other things he knew about the situation. For example, imagine that a scientist gets thousands of exclusively positive results while testing an hypothesis and is sure of the hypothesis. Yet imagine that one result is irrelevant because the wrong materials were used by mistake. We can suppose that the mistake makes no difference, that the other results are sufficient. But imagine that the scientist thinks otherwise and that he would not have been sure had he known of the mistake. Even so, he *is* technically sure of the hypothesis and can know it to be true, his misguided methodology notwithstanding.[1]

Similarly, the counterfactual component of technical sureness does not imply that, if someone would have been sure of something had he considered the matter rationally, he is technically sure of it. Otherwise a very bright person could end up knowing everything entailed by a given proposition he knows. The condition merely implies that, if someone would have been sure had he been governed by reason in whatever considerations he happens to be engaged in, he is technically sure. Granted, someone who would have assented in appropriate circumstances can be said to be technically sure, since sureness is not an occurrence. But to say that someone would have been sure of an entailed proposition had he considered it is not to say that he would have assented to the proposition in a way that discloses that he *is* sure of it. Thus, technical sureness is not that easy a state to attain, in spite of its counterfactual dimension.

Indeed, although technical sureness is in some ways less demanding than sureness in an ordinary sense, technical sureness still makes heavy demands on knowledge. A knower must find that which he knows to be absolutely certain, not just certain for practical purposes. Someone who has purely philosophical doubts therefore fails to be sure and fails to have knowledge. Of course, if his doubts are irrational, he is not on that account unsure. For example, if a junior philosopher in a department of senior sceptics has doubts solely because he wants to get tenure, he is not thereby unsure of anything. But if his doubts are grounded in philosophical reasons, he is unsure and lacks knowledge. Similarly, someone who correctly remembers something, but who reasonably thinks that he is just guessing, fails to be sure of what he remembers. And someone who gets things right because he has psychic powers, but who finds psychic judgments untrustworthy, fails to be sure of his judgments. Demanding technical sureness therefore makes the present concept of knowledge more demanding than most, if not all, ordinary concepts.[2]

Two major sorts of objections might be brought against making technical sureness a condition of knowledge. On the one hand, those who think that knowledge and belief are incompatible might feel that sureness cannot even be coherently stipulated as a requirement of knowledge. On the other hand, those who think that knowledge entails belief might object to constructing a concept of knowledge that can be assigned to someone who disbelieves what he knows.

The Compatibility of Knowledge and Belief

Incompatibilists are right to see striking differences between knowledge and belief. But the differences fall short of establishing a necessary opposition. For example, as Austin points out, we ask "How do you know?" and "Why do you believe?" not "How do you believe?" and "Why do you know?" But we do not ask "How do you true?" and yet this does not make knowledge and truth incompatible. Similarly, the point of "He knows it, he doesn't believe it" is not to disclose friction, but to guard against misleading understatement, as in "He's a grandfather, not a father."

Vendler suggests that if it were possible to know and believe the same thing, there would be a reading for

A knows what B believes.

which parallels the one for

A believes what B believes.

He thinks that no such reading is available.[3] Yet we do have constructions like

B believes what A knows.
What A knows is the same as what B believes.
A knows that which B believes.

These are enough to preserve compatibility.

Vendler also tries to drive a wedge between objects of belief and objects of knowledge. He thinks that beliefs take propositions as objects and that belief contexts are referentially opaque; e.g., "Tully is wise" and "Cicero is wise" are different objects of belief even though Tully and Cicero are the same. On the other hand, he thinks that knowledge takes a fact as object and that knowledge contexts are transparent. Thus, if A both knows and believes that Tully is wise, and B both knows and believes that Cicero is wise, it seems that the object of A's knowledge and belief is both the same as and different from the object of B's knowledge and belief.

Now, such a result might not be as awkward as it first seems. It simply means that, whereas A and B both know that Tully is wise, A alone believes it, which appears harmless. Moreover, it is not clear that knowledge contexts are never opaque. There seems to be a sense in which A alone knows that Tully is wise, given that B does not know that Tully is Cicero. Consequently, we can say that knowledge involves two objects, both a proposition and a fact, and that, whereas the factual objects of A's knowledge and B's knowledge are the same, their propositional objects differ. We can then identify the propositional object of knowledge with an object of belief. The attempt to drive a wedge between the two therefore fails.

The Independence of Knowledge and Belief

Those who think that knowledge necessarily involves belief sometimes argue that considerations that serve to disclose knowledge equally serve to disclose belief, hence that even in a self-deception case whatever discloses the unconscious knowledge also discloses an unconscious belief.[4] But we assign knowledge to a self-deceiver partly because his protests are forced and pitifully defended, partly because he has powerful motives not to assent, partly because he is often suspiciously evasive, and partly because he eventually assents in therapeutic circumstances, conceding that he knew all along but just couldn't accept it. This type of behaviour pattern is best explained by supposing that he knows that which he denies. But there is no need to suppose that he also believes what he denies. Indeed, the knowledge hypothesis works precisely because the knowlege it assigns can be stripped of belief.

Lehrer tries to tie knowledge to belief by arguing that anyone who knows that p and that he says that p must know that he correctly says that p, in which case he must believe that he knows and hence believe what he knows.[5] But a self-deceiver who knows that he is arrogant and jokingly says "I am arrogant" need not know that he correctly says that he is arrogant. He need only know the fact that he jokingly happens to state. And we can't say that this knowledge involves belief without begging the question.

Attempts to link knowledge to being sure in an ordinary sense are even less convincing. Malcolm argues that lack of confidence is taken to be a sign of ignorance, and Cohen that it reveals a lack of expertise.[6] But if someone's hesitation can be explained away as a nervous reaction, and if the contents of his replies to questions and objections are suitably impressive, we can reject the standard signs as misleading. Ayer at one point argues that being sure is necessary for knowledge because "to say of oneself that one knew such and such a statement was true but that one was not altogether sure of it would be self-contradictory."[7] Yet this is precisely what a former self-deceiver can say. Indeed, he can say "I knew it but was convinced of the contrary." Granted, the present-tense "I know it but am sure of the contrary" is self-refuting. But it is not self-contradictory. Thus, the decision to retain nothing more than technical sureness as a requirement of knowledge remains sound, both as a contribution to defining an ideal form of knowledge and as a reflection of some features of ordinary usage.

3. CERTAINTY

What is known must be absolutely certain in the sense defined in chapter 3, section 2. It must be certain in accordance with philosophical standards, not merely practical or discipline-oriented standards. Consequently, we cannot know something if there is good philosophical reason to doubt it, even though for practical purposes such reasons are irrelevant. In this respect the present concept is more demanding than most ordinary concepts.

To guard against the possibility of fortuitous knowledge, we must align the sureness and certainty requirements. For example, suppose that a father is sure of something because of what his son told him. Suppose also that his daughter told him the same thing but, because he does not trust her judgment in such matters, he is not sure of it for this reason. Now, it might be that what he is sure of is not certain given his son's report, because unknown to him the son is trying to deceive him, whereas it is certain given the daughter's report, because unknown to him she does have a good track record in such matters. In that case the father fails to have knowledge, even though he is sure and what he is sure of is certain given his evidence. Thus, we must say that someone knows something only if it is certain *given what makes him sure of it*. If he is sure because he intuits it, it must be intuitively plausible and hence certain for this reason. If he infers it from prior evidence, it must be certain given that prior evidence. If he is sure because of what he observes, it must be certain given what he observes, and so on. This alignment should be implicitly understood in the following discussion.

Imposing certainty on knowledge is tantamount to saying "If he knows, he must be right." Although certainty does not entail epistemic necessity, we cannot justifiably claim that something is certain without being entitled to claim that it is necessary. Thus, if we justifiably assign knowledge to someone, we are justified in saying that what he knows must be the case. This does not mean that we are justified in saying that he must have such knowledge, however. As we shall see in chapter 8, sceptics often assume that absolutely certain knowledge has to embrace both conditions. But the present concept of certainty does not. If there is a connection between the necessity of what one knows and the necessity of one's knowing it, this has to be established by argument. It cannot just be written into the expression's use.

Demanding absolute certainty does set a very high standard for knowledge. Indeed, many would say straight off that the standard is too high to be satisfied except possibly in a few instances. But this is not obviously the case. And the fact that many are dubious about satisfying the standard means that applying it to knowledge does preserve a suitably ambitious ideal. I don't think that we should relinquish it unless we are shown that it is clearly foolhardy.

4. JUSTIFICATION

The combination of being sure and certain is not sufficient for knowledge, even if truth requirements are also satisfied. Imagine that someone is sure that lemons are citrus, that it is certain that they are citrus, given what makes him sure, and that they are in fact citrus. He can still fail to know that they are citrus because he can fail to be justified in being sure. For instance, he might be sure because of what his niece told him, where he lacks information about her reliability in such matters. Imposing this requirement may exceed the demands of ordinary usage. But it helps to strengthen the ideal without putting it clearly beyond our reach.

The expression "justifiably sure" must be understood flexibly in view of the technical use of "sure." Someone can be justifiably sure of something even if he is not sure of it in an ordinary sense, provided he would have been sure, and justifiably so, had he been governed by rational considerations. Moreover, "is justifiably sure" is best taken to mean "is justified in being sure" to avoid implying "is sure."

The justification requirement means that someone who fails to be justified fails to have knowledge. He does not merely lack an entitlement to claim knowledge. Knowledge does to this extent have an iterative dimension. A knower must be justified in claiming the certainty of what he knows. Indeed, it is useful to go ever farther and say that a knower must be justified in claiming knowledge. For convenience, I shall assume that this is a corollary of the condition that a knower must be justifiably sure of what he knows, although, strictly speaking, it is not. But this does not mean that a knower must know that he has knowledge. Any such connection must be established by argument. It is not a deliberate part of the present concept.

Just as the sureness and certainty requirements must be coaligned in order to avoid fortuitous knowledge, so they must be aligned with the justification requirement. For example, someone might be sure of something solely because of report *A*, but be justified in being sure of it solely in view of report *B*. In that case he fails to have knowledge in the present sense. Thus, we must say that someone has knowledge only if he is justifiably sure *in view of what makes him sure*. This qualification should also be implicitly understood in the following discussion.

The justification requirement is not always sharply distinguished from the certainty requirement. For example, when Ayer suggests that a female seer who consistently predicts lottery winners knows the next winner because she has the "right to be sure," he seems to assume both that the prediction is certain given her past record and that she is justifiably sure in view of her past success.[8] It is important to keep the two requirements separate, however, partly for the sake of clarity, partly to offer distinct challenges to scepticism.

Requiring justification as a condition of knowledge does not rule out intuitive knowledge. Suppose that someone finds something intuitively plausible and is sure of it; i.e., he does not derive its plausibility from anything else, nor does he find it plausible because of what he observes or remembers or the like. Suppose that his intuition is correct and that what he is sure of is therefore certain. Finally, suppose that his intuitions are sufficiently reliable that he is justified in being sure. He can then have knowledge, in which case we shall call his knowledge *intuitive*. Thus, if a seer finds it plausible that my lost uncle has escaped to Brazil and she satisfies the remaining conditions of knowing that he is there, the question of whether her knowledge is intuitive depends solely on how she finds such a thing to be plausible. If she finds it plausible *because* it suddenly came to her, she does not thereby find it intuitively plausible, and we must say that her knowledge is *based on* her vision. On the other hand, if she finds it plausible without doing so because of anything else, she finds it intuitively plausible and in that case her knowledge is intuitive.

The justification requirement does not mean that a knower must always be able to justify his position to others. For example, someone might observe a bizarre event in such a way that he is justifiably sure that the event is real, and he might continue to be justifiably sure as he remembers it. But he might not be able to describe his observations and their circumstances in a way that enables anyone else to be justifiably sure. Similarly, a detective might be justifiably sure of a murderer's identity without being able to supply evidence that entitles a jury to be sure. The lack of a shared background can prevent the communication of knowledge.

Although the justification requirement is not designed to make knowledge conform entirely to the demands of ordinary usage, it does not produce a distorting effect. For example, Goldman criticizes a justificationist account on the ground that, whereas we can say in an extended sense that a seeing-eye door knows that an object is approaching, it would be totally absurd to say that the door is justifiably sure of anything.[9] But we *can* say that the door is like someone who sees the approaching object; and if anyone who had seen the object in the given circumstances would have been justifiably sure of its approaching, the door does satisfy something like the justification requirement. Hence we can assign knowledge to the door in an extended sense. Although the ideal concept is special, it still has its roots in ordinary thought.

5. PERMANENT JUSTIFICATION

We can further strengthen the ideal by saying that someone knows something only if he is *permanently* justified in being sure of it, in the sense that, for any addition of new evidence, he would still have been justifiably sure of it in view of what makes him sure. This requirement is needed to allow us to concede that if a sceptic can produce a new argument that destroys our justification for being sure, the sceptic thereby establishes that we never did have knowledge, not merely that we then no longer have it. If we concede this much and then show that a sceptic never will produce such an argument, we defend a claim to have a very demanding form of knowledge.

Insisting that the justification must be permanent does not imply that someone who knows something must continue to be justifiably sure of it. He might lose some of his original evidence and for this reason cease to be justified. The requirement implies that, given that his evidence simply increases, he must continue to be justifiably sure for the same reasons. And the increase can be by accumulating any portion of the absolutely total evidence, however remote in time or space.

It should be made clear, however, that we are talking about evidence that exists somewhere and at some time, not just possible evidence. Permanent justification is a matter of being able to withstand any further evidence that exists. It is not a matter of being able to withstand purely conceivable evidence. For example, suppose that I am permanently justified in being sure that I have two hands, in view of my seeing and feeling two hands at the ends of my arms. This means that there *is* no evidence, had by anyone at any time, such that combining it with my present evidence would defeat my justification for being sure. It does not mean that no such counterevidence is conceivable. For instance, I can conceive of evidence of a divine emissary who reveals a global sensory deception. If this evidence were added to my present evidence, it would discredit my visual and tactile evidence. The mere conceivability of such evidence does not damage the permanence of my justification. It merely establishes the conceivability of my not knowing that I have two hands, not my ignorance. For this reason, we should avoid calling the permanent-justification condition an "indefeasibility condition." The latter expression is sometimes insensitive to the distinction between excluding actual counterevidence and excluding merely possible counterevidence.

Some philosophers think that a permanent-justification condition is too demanding for any relevant ordinary concept of knowledge, and they might adopt a similar attitude toward the ideal concept. The issue is whether some potentially awkward counterevidence is too misleading to deprive anyone of knowledge. For example, Lehrer and Paxson describe a type of case in which a teacher sees a student, Tom, steal a library book, where the teacher is justifiably sure that Tom is stealing the book and where the theft is certain given the teacher's evidence. Unknown to the teacher, Tom's mother will later testify that Tom was not in the library at the time and that his twin brother was. But Tom's mother is a pathological liar and Tom has no twin. According to Lehrer and Paxson, the teacher knows that Tom is the thief, even though the teacher would not have been justifiably sure had he learned of the forthcoming testimony and nothing else.[10]

Now, if the teacher's evidence is strong enough to justify his being sure, one would reasonably expect it to be strong enough to withstand evidence of the mother's testimony and to justify a reply like "She'll be telling a lie—you know what mothers are like." Granted, the teacher has no evidence that Tom has a mother. Hence the teacher has no specific evidence that would discredit her testimony. But sometimes we are justified in rejecting new counterevidence even if we lack specific discrediting evidence. For instance, we can be justifiably sure that people don't survive being sawn in half, observe someone survive being sawn in half on television, and reject what we observe as bad evidence, even though we cannot explain the trick. In the same general way, the teacher could be entitled to reject the mother's testimony as bad evidence, in which case his justification for being sure *is* in this respect permanent and knowledge is possible. On the other hand, if the teacher's evidence would not have thus absorbed evidence of the mother's forthcoming testimony, his justification is not permanent and he fails to have knowledge. For instance, suppose that evidence of the testimony can be supported by independent evidence of a twin's presence in the library and that the teacher would not have been justified in rejecting this augmented counterevidence. In that case the teacher does not know for sure that Tom is the thief. True, operating with such a concept of knowing does invite sceptical objections. But as long as there is a decent chance that the objections are mistaken, we should construct a concept that does precisely that.

Similar remarks apply to a type of problem case offered by Harman, in which a woman, Jill, reads of an assassination in a reliable newspaper, where the story is true but, unknown to her, high-ranking officials try to broadcast a denial in order to restore order. Harman agrees that if the denial is actually broadcast, Jill fails to know of the assassination. But he thinks that, if a mechanical breakdown prevents the message from reaching the public, Jill has knowledge, even though had she learned of the attempted broadcast and nothing else she would not have been justifiably sure.[11]

If Jill is justifiably sure of the assassination in view of the newspaper report, there is a good chance that she would have been justified in saying "They must be lying" had she learned of the attempted broadcast, even though she has no independent discrediting evidence. If this is the extent of the counterevidence she lacks, it is probably not strong enough to violate the permanent-justification condition, which is why her knowing remains possible. On the other hand, if there is also evidence that the officials were just as close to the scene as the reporter who wrote the newspaper article, that they have been generally honest, and that they had no good reason to expect riots by an informed public, we can assume that Jill would not have been justifiably sure of the assassination had she obtained this evidence. But then she does not know that the assassination occurred. Thus, a violation of the permanent-justification condition coincides with a failure to have knowledge. Indeed, this coincidence serves to explain why Jill is ignorant in a case where the denial is actually broadcast. There are then masses of people who disbelieve the assassination, and, had she learned of this, she presumably would not have been entitled to reject the broadcast as bad counterevidence without specific discrediting evidence.

6. TRUTH

The condition that any proposition must be true—given that knowing its negation would have destroyed a knower's justification for being sure of what he knows—implies, among other things, that knowledge requires the truth of what is known. There is nothing particularly awkward about this implication. It means that we must be prepared to talk of fictional truth if we talk of fictional knowledge; e.g., we must say "It is true that Macbeth is ambitious" if we say "He knows that Macbeth is ambitious." Moreover, we must take a claim like "Abelard knew that men couldn't fly in machines" to imply "It was true that men couldn't fly then." But no problem of substance emerges from such results.

The truth condition requires more than the truth of what is known, however. For example, in the library theft case, the condition implies that the proposition "Tom has no twin in the library at the time" is true, since knowledge of its negation would have destroyed the teacher's justification for being sure. And note that the condition requires the *truth* of the proposition, not merely strong supporting evidence. Even if the teacher's evidence justifies believing that Tom has no twin, the teacher fails to know that Tom is the thief if Tom does in fact have a twin in the library. Granted, as Almeder points out, this creates the possibility of undetectable ignorance, since Tom could in principle have a twin even though our evidence always justified being sure that he does not.[12] Yet there is nothing wrong with such a possibility. Almeder rejects it on the Austinian ground that we should never accuse anyone of ignorance unless we can offer specific reasons for doubt. But it is theoretically possible for someone to *be* ignorant even though we cannot legitimately accuse him of it, and this objection fails. Of course, some may feel that by imposing a comprehensive truth condition on knowledge we simply play into a sceptic's hands. But all we are doing is offering the sceptic a good card. We are not conceding him the trick.

Harman feels that a comprehensive truth condition does automatically concede victory to the sceptic. He argues that there will always be a proposition that violates the requirement. For example, suppose that a knowledge claimant is sure that *p*, and suppose that *k* is a true proposition predicting the winner in a large, fair lottery. The disjunction *k v not p* is then true. According to Harman, had the claimant learned of the disjunction's truth and nothing else, he would not have been justifiably sure that *p*, since *k* is antecedently improbable and therefore *not p* would be probable. If so, the comprehensive truth condition is violated by the disjunction's negation. And a suitable disjunction can be found for any knowledge claim.[13]

The argument is wrong to assume that the incremental discovery of the disjunction would have left everything else unchanged, especially *k*'s status. If someone who is justifiably sure that *p* had in addition learned that *k v not p*, he would on that account have been justifiably sure that *k*, which means that he would not have failed to be justifiably sure that *p*. Harman tries to block this step by making *k* antecedently improbable. But once independent evidence favours the ticket named in *k* over other tickets, the principle of indifference cannot be applied to establish *k*'s improbability. And combining the cases for *p* and *k v not p* produces an independent case for *k*. Thus, learning of the true disjunction would not have defeated the justification for being sure that *p* and the truth requirement is still satisfied.

Some philosophers think that a comprehensive truth condition cannot do justice to ordinary language. Their concern has no direct application here, since we are not trying to preserve ordinary usage. But we should ensure that their arguments do not create implicit problems for an account of ideal knowledge. Accordingly, I shall pretend that their objections are raised at the ideal level and consider their merit in that light.

Sosa describes a case in which John is justifiably sure that *pvq* solely because he deduces it from *p*, where *p* is false and *q* true. John then justifiably deduces *p v q v r*. Intuitively, *p*'s falsity seems to prevent John from knowing either disjunction. But Sosa wonders whether the comprehensive truth condition can preserve such a result for the triple disjunction. The condition says that John fails to know that $p \lor q \lor r$ if, had he *(ceteris paribus)* known that p is false, he would not have been justifiably sure that $p \lor q \lor r$. Sosa wonders whether under the *ceteris paribus* clause we can suppose that John is still justifiably sure that $p \lor q$. If we can, John would not have failed to be justifiably sure of the triple disjunction, in which case he does not violate the truth requirement.[14]

Sosa's wonder underestimates the demands of the *ceteris paribus* clause. The clause implies that nothing else is to be supposed except John's knowing that p is false *and* anything else logically required by such a change. In this case his learning of p's falsity necessarily would have destroyed his justification for being sure that $p \lor q,$ in which case that consequence must be included in the supposition as well. Hence he would not have been justifiably sure that $p \lor q \lor r$ and the truth condition is violated, in line with our intuitions.

Sosa describes another case in which John is justifiably sure that an animal in front of him is a chameleon, from which he justifiably infers that the animal has a deceptive appearance. Although the animal is a chameleon, it is also wearing a chameleon suit such that, even if it had been a salamander, it would have looked exactly like a chameleon. Intuitively, John does not seem to know either that the animal is a chameleon or that it has a deceptive appearance. Yet Sosa wonders whether the case does violate the comprehensive truth condition in both respects. We might be inclined to say that, had John known that the animal is wearing a cleverly designed chameleon suit, he would still have been justifiably sure that it has a deceptive appearance, in which case he does not violate the truth requirement and knowledge is not ruled out.[15]

There are two reasons for rejecting this line of reasoning. First, even if an enlightened John would still have been justifiably sure that the animal has a deceptive appearance, he would not have been so in view of what makes him sure that the animal has a deceptive appearance, viz., his being sure that it is a chameleon. Hence the truth requirement is violated, since it must be aligned with the sureness, certainty, and justification requirements of knowledge. Second, there is a pun on "deceptive appearance." John is sure that the animal has a deceptive appearance in the sense that he is sure that its colour at a given time is no indication of what its subsequent colour will be, whereas he would have been sure that it has a deceptive appearance only in the sense that he would have been sure that it can easily appear to be a chameleon when it is not. Hence the truth requirement fails to be satisfied.

Clark describes a case in which John is justifiably sure of the propositions

(1) $(pvq) \supset r$
(2) p
(3) $(not\text{-}p.s) \supset q$
(4) $not\text{-}s \supset p$

Suppose that John is justifiably sure that r solely because he deduces it from (1) and (2). He does not realize that r is also entailed by the conjunction of (1), (3), and (4). Suppose that p is false. Intuitively, John seems not to know that r. But even if he had known that p is false, he would still have been justified in being sure that r, since r is entailed by (1), (3), and (4). Hence, it might seem, John does not violate the comprehensive-truth condition.[16] But contrary to appearances, he does violate the condition, since he would not have been justified in being sure that r in view of what makes him sure that r, viz., his being sure that p. The necessary alignment is missing. Consequently, the truth requirement still preserves our intuitions.

Locke describes a case in which we know that Jones is in pain because we find him bleeding, writhing, and groaning, even though Jones is a practical joker and had we known this, we would not have been sure that he is in pain.[17] But this does not violate the truth requirement. If, given knowledge of Jones's character, our evidence would still have justified our being sure that he is in pain, the requirement is satisfied and we know that he is in pain. Our counterfactual subjective response is irrelevant.

There are situations in which someone who is justifiably sure that p would not have been justified had he known that q is false because *by parity of reasoning* a failure in justification for q dictates a like failure for p. For example, imagine that we are justifiably sure that p solely because a reliable source tells us that both p and q. Had we known that q is false, we would not have been justifiably sure that p either. Let us say that our justification for being sure that p is then *comparable* to our justification for being sure that q. Anything that defeats one equally defeats the other.

The comprehensive truth condition of knowledge has the following corollary:

> Nothing that justifies someone in being sure of what he knows can be comparable to a justification for being sure of something false.

Discovery of such a false proposition would have defeated the justification for being sure of the proposition and hence by parity of reasoning would have defeated the justification for being sure of what is allegedly known. Thus a violation of the corollary is a violation of the truth requirement.

Some philosophers are suspicious of such a corollary. Sosa describes a case in which a congenitally blind man is justifiably sure that his wife is both beautiful and vain because he constantly hears her praise herself. Although she is not beautiful, she is vain, and Sosa thinks that the man can know this, even though his evidence also justifies being sure of something false.[18] Now, whether the case violates the corollary depends upon whether the man's justification for being sure of his wife's vanity is comparable to his justification for being sure of her beauty. If the justifications are comparable, evidence against her beauty equally counts against her vanity. In other words, his case for her vanity is then inextricably tied to his case for her beauty. But in that event her failure to be beautiful is a reason to think that he does not know that she is vain. Consequently, violation of the corollary is not an embarrassment. On the other hand, if the two justifications are not comparable, the corollary is unviolated and the man is free to know that his wife is vain.

The corollary should be distinguished from the excessively harsh condition that nothing that justifies someone's being sure of what he knows can justify his being sure of something false. Suppose that a true e justifies someone's being sure of a true e', which in turn justifies his being sure of a false q. Since justification is transitive, e justifies his being sure of the false q. Yet it seems possible for him to know that e' on the basis of e. This much is correct.[19] But the case does not violate the given corollary. Even if the subject had learned of $q's$ falsity, he still could have been justifiably sure that e, or that e'. For example, e' might consist in his being told that q and e consist in his hearing someone tell him that q. Even if he had learned that q is false, he still could have been justifiably sure that he was told that q or that he heard someone tell him. The corollary does not say that a knower's justification cannot underwrite falsity. It merely says that a knower's justification cannot underwrite falsity in such a way that discovering the falsity would have damaged the justification. Such a requirement *is* demanding, but not so demanding that it completely fails to respect ordinary intuitions.

7. SUMMARY

Ideally, our knowing something involves four things: our being sure of it, the certainty of what we are sure of, our being permanently justified in being sure of it, and the truth of propositions essential to that justification. Although the concept governed by these four conditions is more demanding than ordinary concepts, the demands are not so great that they distort our intellectual aspirations. Nor do they put knowledge unarguably beyond our reach. Thus, the question of whether we have knowledge is the question of whether these four conditions are satisfied. This will be our topic in the remaining chapters.

The Justification of Knowledge Claims

Strategy

1. A CARTESIAN APPROACH

Are we ever justified in claiming knowledge in the sense defined in the previous chapter? I think that we are, but only if we can answer major philosophical objections. For example, claiming knowledge involves claiming that something is absolutely certain, and we cannot justifiably claim certainty unless we can answer otherwise attractive arguments for universal doubt. Similarly, claiming knowledge involves claiming that something is absolutely true, and we cannot justifiably claim absolute truth unless we are able to meet a sceptic's charge that absolute truth is inaccessible. Justification is impossible in a philosophical vacuum.

Since knowing involves being justified in claiming knowledge, knowing involves developing an ability to cope with scepticism. In other words, no one knows anything unless he has actually done some philosophy. Uneducated common sense is not enough. Thus, in answering scepticism I am not playing the underlabourer's role of defending a claim to have an antecedently acquired knowledge. An investigation of the merits of scepticism is itself an essential part of the process of discovery. Descartes holds such a view in his struggle with scepticism and to that extent the present approach is Cartesian (although in other respects it is quite different).

2. SHORTER APPROACHES

Evaluating specific sceptical arguments is a lengthy, and in some ways a risky, venture. As a result, some may prefer to take a shorter route. But I doubt that effective shortcuts are available.

Moore tries a shorter way when he accuses a sceptic of self-refutation, e. g., of claiming to know that there are human beings who never know whether other minds exist.[1] But a sceptic in the present sense need only disclaim ideal knowledge of other minds, which leaves him free to claim practical knowledge of their existence. Or he is free to claim that a belief in other minds is justified, while denying that we are justifiably sure of their existence. Or if his scepticism also undermines justified belief, he can still consistently believe in the existence of other minds, provided he concedes that he has no justification for holding this belief rather than its opposite.

Moore tries another shortcut when he responds to doubts about whether he has a hand by saying, "You might as well suggest that I do not know that I am now standing up and talking."[2] But that is precisely what a consistent sceptic *is* suggesting. The only effective way to counter the suggestion is to examine his reasons, not to dismiss his view out of hand.

Moore may be offering a third shortcut when he suggests that we can always respond to sceptical arguments by appealing to the greater antecedent worth of ordinary knowledge claims.[3] Now, if he is merely suggesting that, having examined a sceptic's premises, we can judge them to be worth less than the knowledge claims they purport to undermine, his methodology is unproblematic. But if he is suggesting that we are somehow *compelled* to give this sort of answer to any sceptical argument, whatever its content, his approach is untenable. There is no reason to think that the antecedent case for ordinary-knowledge claims is bound to be stronger than a proposed sceptical argument. There is always a real chance that the latter argument will succeed.

Malcolm sees a different type of shortcut in Moore's position. According to Malcolm, we can always cite the fact that knowledge-ascribing sentences have a proper use, to protect them from the sceptic's charge of being logically absurd, and we can do so quite independently of a sceptic's supporting arguments.[4] Now, it is obvious that knowledge-ascribing sentences have a proper use only in the sense that they are syntactically correct and the words they contain are used in proper senses. But in this sense of "proper use," the sentence "He drank the number 2" is also used properly, even though what it says is logically absurd. On the other hand, if the expression "proper use" deliberately excludes logical absurdity, it is not obvious that knowledge-ascribing sentences do have a proper use, or at least it is not so obvious that sceptical attempts to show otherwise should be ignored. Thus, Malcolm's argument either fails to counter scepticism or fails to show that sceptical arguments should not be considered on their merits.

Wittgenstein hints at a short way with scepticism when he suggests that sceptical doubts cannot be consistently formulated by anyone who knows what he means by what he says.[5] But a sceptic can know what his words mean, in the sense of being able to use them, and yet not know what they mean, in the sense of not being able to describe authoritatively what they mean. And he needs only the first kind of knowledge in order to formulate his position. Moreover, a sceptic need only doubt things in the sense of insisting that the opposite may be the case. Hence he only needs to say "These words may not have any meaning," which is not a heavy cost. Thus, if confronted by Wittgenstein's remark,

> If you tried to doubt everything you would not get as far as doubting anything. The game of doubting itself presupposes certainty.[6]

a sceptic can draw a distinction between doubting and denying, concede that he is not denying everything, and argue that doubting everything is perfectly coherent. We may not agree with his conclusions. But that is to challenge his arguments, not to circumvent them.

Against this view, Prichard maintains that, even when doubt is distinguished from denial, a universal doubt is incoherent. He thinks that "we can only be uncertain of one thing because we are certain of something else, and therefore to maintain, as the sceptic does, that we are uncertain of everything is impossible."[7] But someone can be selective in his scepticism; e.g., he can claim to be certain of his own existence while disclaiming certainty concerning external objects. And we still have to attend to these sceptical arguments. Moreover, there is nothing obviously right about Prichard's position. It seems that a sceptic can coherently say "This may not be true, since p is the case, and of course p may not be true either, precisely because p is the case."

Now, someone might defend Prichard by arguing that a universal reason for doubt eventually becomes a universal reason for nonacceptance, given that a conclusion's uncertainty increases when its support is also uncertain. For example, suppose that a material-object proposition is doubtful, its support is doubtful, the support for its support is doubtful, and so on. It might be argued that the doubt that attaches to the material-object proposition is steadily increased by the doubt that in turn infects each support, to a point where we should refuse to accept the proposition. If this holds for every proposition, a sceptic then has no acceptable starting point, in which case perhaps we should not bother with his arguments.

But since the ground for doubting the proposition and its support is the same universal ground, there is no independent ground for doubting the support. Hence there is no compounding of doubt for this reason. Moreover, a philosophical ground for doubt does not usually assign a numerical probability to a material-object proposition, a value that can be mechanically diminished if the proposition's support has a value less than 1.0. Thus, there is no increase for this reason either. Furthermore, it follows that a philosophical ground does not usually assign numerical values to each of the ordered supports for the proposition, values that can then be multiplied to produce a much lower value for their conjunction. Finally, even if the proposition's uncertainty were increased by the uncertainty of its ordered supports, it need not increase to a point where we should refuse to accept it, given that the chain of supports is finite and reasonably short. Thus, a sceptic who doubts even his own ground for doubt still adopts a coherent position.[8]

Attempts to short-cut scepticism are like attempts to win a victory without fighting any major battles. The only way to make progress is to engage the sceptic in combat. Of course, this implies that he may be the one who wins in the end. But that is precisely the way things are—there is a real chance that the sceptic is right. Now, some might feel that to concede this much is already to concede defeat. But to assess such a feeling is to enter the battle, not to discuss strategy. Accordingly, I shall spend the next two chapters examining the concession and its implications for claiming knowledge.

CHAPTER SEVEN

Toleration

1. INTRODUCTION

I am prepared to concede the following possibilities to scepticism: In every, or virtually every, given case, good counterevidence may exist; justification-defeating evidence may exist; and anything that is absolutely certain may not really be certain. In other words, it is never, or almost never, certain that something is certain, and we never, or almost never, know that we have knowledge. Concessions of this sort express an attitude of *epistemological toleration,* and we can call the refusal to make such concessions *dogmatism.* A dogmatist is therefore neither someone who holds a view for no good reason nor someone who is resolved to retain a view come what may. He is someone who holds a philosophical theory, viz., that we are sometimes entitled to claim that good counterevidence is impossible, or that we can sometimes be justifiably sure that something is certain. He need not be dogmatic in a pejorative sense.

Toleration seems to be so clearly right that I have deliberately not added a dogmatic requirement to the concept of ideal knowledge. Knowledge has not been defined to require a knower to be sure that he knows, nor has it been defined to require the impossibility of good counterevidence, or the certainty that what is known is absolutely certain. True, a form of knowledge that satisfies dogmatic requirements would be more desirable than one that does not. But it seems so obvious that such requirements cannot be satisfied that imposing them on knowledge would make it a completely unrealistic ideal. Consequently, I have decided to omit them from the concept.

Three considerations support a tolerant assertion of knowledge claims.

First, sometimes when we are justifiably sure of something, new evidence subsequently turns up to destroy our justification. For example, new evidence sometimes forces the reversal of a guilty verdict in a murder trial, even though the original verdict was justified. Thus, in any instance where we are now justifiably sure of something, there is a chance that new evidence will overturn our claim to have knowledge. This can be called the *frequency argument* for toleration.

Second, it is always possible to improve our justification for being sure. For instance, someone who places a large bet on what he justifiably takes to be a sure thing can still consistently check to ensure that the evidence is as solid as he thinks it is. He can seek confirmation in this sense. But if a check can confirm his assessment of the evidence, it can equally disconfirm it. Hence the possibility of improvement involves the equal possibility of refutation.

Third, although philosophical arguments for disclaiming certainty have thus far been unsuccessful, they retain enough merit to force the concession that some of them just may turn out to be sound. A sceptic deserves to be taken seriously even if we disagree with him. Consequently, there always may be good philosophical reason for withdrawing a knowledge claim.

Nevertheless, the case for toleration is not so obvious that it is beyond philosophical criticism. There are philosophers who think that we can and should be dogmatic in the present sense. I shall therefore examine some dogmatic responses in this chapter before considering the significance of toleration in the next.

2. SELF-GUARANTEEING PROPOSITIONS

Suppose that a dogmatist appeals to the proposition "There is good counterevidence in the universe." There cannot be good evidence against it, since the existence of such evidence would verify it. Nevertheless, there may be a good ground to doubt it, since there may be a proof that shows that the existence of a good ground for doubt does not entail the existence of good counterevidence. This much toleration is still coherent. Moreover, even if we can be dogmatic about this particular proposition, we have no reason to extend the attitude any farther. Very little can be derived from the proposition; and because of the distinctive way it resists possible refutation, it cannot serve as a fruitful paradigm.

Somewhat similar remarks apply to "I exist." I can never have counterevidence unless the proposition is true. But there may still be good counterevidence that does not require anyone to have it; e.g., there may be good evidence against the coherence of personal pronouns. If a dogmatist then strips "I" of descriptive content, and uses it simply as a referential label, there may still be good evidence against the existence of entities of any sort. If a dogmatist then refuses to commit the proposition to the existence of an entity, he transforms it into the absolutely minimal "There is something." But the latter says so little that it is entailed by every proposition except "There is nothing," including propositions like "There is a contradiction" and "There is an adjective." Thus, the stock of propositions that invite a dogmatic attitude remains very small.[1]

3. CONVENTIONALLY GUARANTEED PROPOSITIONS

Suppose that either we agree to use the word "centre" as a synonym for "middle," or this usage is endorsed by general convention. If we accordingly say "A centre is a middle," good counterevidence is impossible. The governing convention rules out the possibility of any development that shows that something is a centre but not a middle. The very identity of the given proposition is such that, necessarily, anything that shows that x is not a middle automatically shows that x is not a centre. Consequently, we *can* be dogmatic about conventionally guaranteed propositions.

This is not a disturbing result. Although conventionally guaranteed propositions are legislatively immune to refutation, they are on that very account not proper objects of knowledge. When we claim to know something, we imply the absence of good counterevidence. We thereby presuppose that the absence of such evidence is a matter for assertion, an assertion that may need defending. But if a proposition is conventionally guaranteed, there is no room for such an assertion. Merely by considering the proposition, we adopt a convention that decides the matter. Thus, the claim "I know that a centre is a middle" makes the absence of good counterevidence a matter both for decision and for assertion. Claiming knowledge in this case is like saying "I now know what I shall do" in a way that ignores the distinction between recording a decision and making a prediction. Thus, the fact that some propositions are conventionally guaranteed does not mean that we can be dogmatic about propositions of which we can justifiably claim knowledge.[2]

4. NECESSARY TRUTHS

Some think that we can at least be dogmatic about elementary equations. For example, Malcolm says that even if several intelligent people earnestly claimed to have disproven $2 + 2 = 4$, and even if he couldn't see anything wrong with the disproof, he would still refuse to abandon the equation.[3] Now, such an attitude can be justified to some extent. Our justification for accepting an equation can be sufficiently strong that even if we cannot spot an error in a purported disproof, we are still entitled on general grounds not to accept the disproof as good evidence. But this is not to endorse a dogmatic attitude. It does not mean that there are no possible circumstances in which retaining the equation would be unjustified. For instance, if we examined the proof several times, consulted good mathematicians, and our intuitions then started to waver, we would not be justified in holding on to the equation. These are possible developments and therefore dogmatism is still unsupported.

Hempel similarly argues against the possibility of an empirical refutation of $3 + 2 = 5$, on the ground that the numerals and operators are defined to make the equation hold.[4] Now, if this is in effect to say that the equation is conventionally guaranteed against refutation, an empirical refutation *is* impossible. But by the same token, a claim to know the equation's truth is then misplaced. On the other hand, if it means that the truth of the equation is a product of how we define the given expressions, the point is mistaken. Although the identity of the equation depends on what the expressions mean, and although the impossibility of good counterevidence can be dictated by the way the expressions are used, the truth of the equation is a matter of whether things are as the equation asserts them to be. The equation is true just insofar as $3 + 2 = 5$. Thus, once we agree that the equation is not a conventionally guaranteed proposition, we have no basis for rejecting the possibility of good counterevidence, including empirical counterevidence.

Hempel thinks that, for any apparent counterevidence, supplementary moves will be made to protect the equation from refutation. For instance, if we ostensibly count three microbes, then two more, and then a total of six microbes, he thinks that we would assume that either we had made a mistake or that one microbe had split. This much is correct. But if in addition our intuitions changed, if mathematicians all rejected the equation, if we kept getting a total of six microbes, and if there was no evidence of splitting, our reaction probably would be quite different. And these are also possible developments.[5]

This does not mean that elementary equations are therefore empirical. Although they are subject to empirical disconfirmation, they can still be known *a priori*, in the sense that they can be found to be intuitively plausible, or their plausibility can be derived from something intuitively plausible. We need not find them plausible because of what we sense, or observe, or remember. The expression *"a priori"* is generally sensitive to the way something is found to be plausible, not to the way the remaining conditions of justified acceptance are satisfied. This is why *a priori* philosophical propositions can still be vulnerable to empirical counterexamples and can still be confirmed by peer acceptance.

Avoiding a dogmatic attitude toward given propositions does not involve forsaking their logically necessary truth. In conceding that there may be good counterevidence, we are saying something about the state of the evidence that bears on a proposition. We are not saying anything about the proposition's truth. The possibility of good counterevidence does not entail the logical possibility of the proposition's being false. The remark "There may be good reason to doubt that 3 + 2 necessarily equals 5" does not imply "It is logically possible for 3 + 2 not to equal (or not to have equalled) 5." The former remark merely indicates that there may not be a conclusive case for finding the equation necessarily true, which does not mean that the equation is not a necessary truth.[6]

This does imply that some necessary truths are revisable in a way that does not involve a change in meaning. Grice and Strawson try to preserve the analyticity of some necessary truths by holding that they are subject only to conceptual revision, i.e., that we can merely alter the statement being made, not reasonably disbelieve the given statement.[7] For example, they think that anyone who denies "A three-year-old child is not an adult" must either fail to understand the words or be proposing a new meaning for them. Now, it *is* possible to use such words in a way that conventionally guarantees the resulting statement against refutation, and in that case the Grice-Strawson analysis applies. But not all necessary truths are conventionally guaranteed. And even the words in the given sentence can be so used that there is no guarantee against refutation. For instance, I can make the remark in a way that lets me coherently wonder whether an effective counterexample is provided by a case where a three-year-old undergoes a radical transformation every six hours, alternating between babbling in a playpen and developing philosophical theories. The fact that the question is open as to whether the case provides a counterexample establishes the possibility of good counterevidence and hence of genuine refutation.

A dogmatic attitude should be avoided even in the case of very fundamental necessary truths. For example, it is possible that there are good grounds for doubting the law of noncontradictions—e.g., grounds that cite liar-paradoxical sentences. Nagel distrusts carrying toleration to such lengths. He doubts that a logical law can be put to a suitably independent test, since he feels that no description of a test case will be accepted unless it abides by the law being tested.[8] But not every description of a liar-paradoxical sentence that portrays it as involving a genuine contradiction is inadmissible just on that account. Granted, as things now stand, we are justified in rejecting the description even if we cannot diagnose where it goes wrong. But this does not mean that the description could never be sustained in a way that would defeat our justification. A tolerant attitude should be preserved even when our most sacred assumptions are involved.

5. SUBJECTIVE REPORTS

Let us assume that first-person reports of current mental states are more than just the minimal "There is something" and that they are not just conventionally guaranteed against refutation. Otherwise they offer no distinct challenge to a tolerant epistemology. Some philosophers feel that we can be dogmatic about at least some subjective reports. For example, Pollock thinks that a sensory report like "I am appeared to that way" has meaning only if "that way" actually refers to something and hence only if the report is true.[9] If he is right, it might seem that the report could never be refuted, since its being refuted implies that it is meaningful and hence true. But the report may be refuted in conjunction with evidence that breaks the connection between being refuted and being meaningful, in which case the refutation would not confirm the report's truth. Moreover, it is not clear that the report's being meaningful requires it to be true. The report is meaningful, we might agree, only if there is a referent for "that way." But it is true only if, in addition, the descriptive expression "appeared to" applies to someone. And it is possible that there is good evidence against applying any such description. Consequently, a refutation is still possible.

The same remark holds in the event that there is a logical link between a report's being accepted by the subject and its being true. Unless the logical link is irrefutable, there may be counterevidence that breaks the connection and combines with further evidence to overthrow the report. For example, suppose that John sincerely reports seeing red but he is not looking at anything red, no one else in the situation sees red, nothing in his brain correlates with seeing red, and he has an ulterior motive for thinking of himself as someone who sees red. Even if his making the report entails that he does see red, there may be good reason to doubt such an entailment, in which case there would be good reason to doubt the report. Hence the report should not be made dogmatically.

Malcolm thinks that external evidence can never make an after-image report doubtful, provided the report is not amended or cancelled by the subject himself. Imagine that someone who reports seeing a seven-pointed after-image draws a six-pointed shape when asked to draw what he sees. If the subject insists that both the report and the drawing are accurate, then according to Malcolm we cannot choose between them—although he admits that they cannot both be right.[10] But in that event the report is not something of which the subject can be justifiably sure—it has been refuted to that extent. Moreover, if the stimulus object has six points, if others in the same situation report seeing six-pointed after-images, if the subject is better at drawing than at counting, if he does not attend carefully to what he sees when he gives his report, and if his brain states correlate with seeing a six-pointed shape, there *is* decent evidence that the report is wrong. Since this sort of evidence is possible for any report, no report should be made dogmatically.

6. RUBBISH

Wittgenstein thinks that there are irrefutable propositions and that we should say "Rubbish!" to anyone who denies them, although he also thinks that they are not proper objects of knowledge claims. Such a view makes sense when applied to conventionally guaranteed propositions. But he has a much larger class in mind. If he is right, we are entitled to be dogmatic about many propositions, including Moorean common-sense propositions like

"The earth has existed for over a hundred years" and "Cats do not grow on trees."[11] Yet he says nothing to support such an attitude.

For example, he suggests that doubting a common-sense proposition would by parity of reasoning plunge everything into chaos.[12] But, although doubting such a proposition on the evidence that we actually have would produce general chaos, doubting it as a result of a change in evidence would not. And toleration merely involves acknowledging that evidential change is possible. For instance, Wittgenstein says, "If I were contradicted on all sides and told this person's name was not what I had always known it was . . . the foundations of all judging would be taken away from me."[13] But if I were impressively contradicted, that very fact would establish a significant difference from the present situation and allow me to disclaim knowledge of the person's name while preserving my other judgments.

He suggests that any set of beliefs contains propositions that cannot be rejected without rejecting the whole set, that disagreements at bedrock create a need to convert rather than to refute. For instance, he thinks that if a queen were brought up in the belief that the world began when she did, a common-sense philosopher like Moore could not prove to the queen that she is wrong; Moore would have to convert her to a different way of looking at the world.[14] Now, getting the queen to concede a mistake would be a large, perhaps a psychologically impossible, task. But that is not the issue. The issue is whether it is possible for Moore to introduce evidence that, even when conjoined with the queen's evidence, justifies holding that her belief is wrong. By the same token, the issue is whether it is possible for her to do the same in reverse. Both developments are possible, even if neither adversary would actually concede defeat; and conceding the error in such circumstances would not require abandoning everything else. Although it might require very extensive revisions, it creates no theoretical problems as long as it leaves something intact.

Wittgenstein also suggests that we can adopt a position where we are simply not ready to let anything count as a disproof of the proposition "I have two hands." I think he is right. This sort of dogmatic attitude is possible. But the question is whether it is ever justified. He suggests that it is, on the ground that it is impossible for me to test the claim to know that I have two hands. He is right to think that the possibility of disproof requires the possibility of subjecting the knowledge claim to a genuine test. But he is wrong to think that a test is impossible. I can test the claim by looking at my hands. He denies that I can because "my having two hands is not less certain before I have looked at them than afterwards."[15] But this confuses a test of the knowledge claim with a test of the proposition known. Although my observation cannot improve the status of the proposition "I have two hands," it can improve the status of the knowledge claim "I know that I have two hands." If this sort of improvement is possible, so is a negative result. Hence we are not entitled to be dogmatic.

Finally, he suggests that in the case of a proposition like "My name is such and such," we can say that, if any apparently good grounds for doubt were introduced, "there would certainly also be something that made the grounds of these doubts themselves seem doubtful," thereby allowing us to preserve our belief.[16] But how can we say that there would *certainly* be such discrediting evidence? We can say that there probably would be some. But the existence of unexpected refutations of other apparently solid beliefs prevents us from being sure. The possibility remains that there is a genuinely good ground for doubt. Therefore attempts to cast doubt on common-sense propositions should not be treated as rubbish.

7. SUMMARY

I have defended a tolerant epistemology as a means of giving the sceptic his due. Arguments for toleration manage to survive dogmatic appeals to self-guaranteeing propositions, conventionally guaranteed propositions, necessary truths, analytic truths, and subjective reports. Moreover, they stand up in the face of Wittgenstein's attempts to dismiss challenges to common sense as rubbish.

Yet perhaps in trying to give the sceptic his due, I have gone too far. Retaining a tolerant attitude may actually sow the seeds of scepticism. Some philosophers feel that we cannot concede the possibility of refutation without on that account rejecting absolute certainty. If they are right, there is no middle way. We are then confronted by a need to choose between dogmatism and scepticism. Let us now see whether the choice is inescapable.

CHAPTER EIGHT

Remaining Sure

1. TOLERATION WITHOUT DOUBT

In the last chapter I gave three reasons for adopting a tolerant epistemology. Briefly, they were, first, that even in optimum circumstances new evidence has sometimes defeated our justification for being sure; second, that the ever-present possibility of improving a justification also involves the ever-present possibility of its being defeated; and third, that sceptical arguments are sufficiently respectable that some of them may be right. The question now is whether any of the three arguments leads ultimately to scepticism. Let us consider them in reverse order.

RESPECT FOR SCEPTICISM

Suppose that a sceptic introduces the Cartesian hypothesis of a powerful and clever demon who deceives us even when we are absolutely sure of things. The sceptic might argue that if we do concede that he may be right, we thereby concede that the demon hypothesis may be correct. Given such a concession, we cannot be justifiably sure of anything, since then each given belief may be false and hence each fails to be absolutely certain. But in conceding that the sceptic may be right, we are not conceding that the demon hypothesis may be correct. We concede that the sceptic's *modal claim* "There may be a demon" may be right, not that the hypothesis "There is a demon" may be right. Thus, we are not conceding that each given belief may be false, only that there may be some good reason to think that it may be false, which is toleration and not scepticism.

This means that we do not have to put the demon hypothesis on a par with common-sense propositions. In saying that there may be a good reason to accept the hypothesis, we are not saying that there *is* such a reason. And in fact there is no such reason—e.g., no reliable authorities accept the hypothesis; it explains nothing that needs explaining; and it is not intuitively attractive. Thus, a tolerant attitude still allows us to accept the challenge to defend common-sense beliefs. For instance, we can argue: It is intuitively plausible that I feel two hands. It is therefore derivatively plausible that hands exist. There is no good ordinary reason to distrust my experience or to deny that hands exist. If a sceptic says "But there may be a demon, hence the experience may be unveridical," his conjecture is gratuitous, since possibility claims need support, and it has none. Consequently, there are the best of reasons for thinking that hands exist. Although the sceptic may be right, in fact he is wrong.[1]

The Possibility of Improvement

Imagine that I have just had a local anaesthetic and don't feel my hands. If I remember the anaesthetic, I can still be justifiably sure that my hands exist, even if I'm not looking at them. But if a lot depends upon whether my hands exist, I might take a peek, not to make sure that they do exist, but to improve the reliability of my evidence and thereby strengthen my justification for being sure. In this sense I can make doubly sure. This sort of improvement is always possible. For instance, even though I currently feel my hands, I can still improve my justification by taking a look or by checking with someone else.

In so doing, however, I do not become justified in being surer than I initially was. I become more justified in being sure. Moreover, that I have hands is as certain given my initial evidence as it is given my subsequent evidence. What changes is my justification for finding such a thing certain. Thus, my having hands need not be less than absolutely certain prior to the improvement, and the possibility of future improvement does not imply that my having hands is now less than absolutely certain. Once again, toleration avoids generating scepticism.[2]

The Frequency Argument

Since there have been unexpected refutations in apparently safe situations, a refutation in any given situation is always possible. Malcolm distrusts such an argument and likens it to arguing, "Francis Bacon may not be English, since some men are not English."[3] But the Bacon argument fails because there is independent evidence that bears on whether Bacon is English, whereas there is no independent evidence as to whether good counterevidence exists, apart from the previous performance of the given type of evidence. Consequently, a frequency argument does work in favour of toleration.

Yet if this much is right, must we then accept the following argument for scepticism?

> Sometimes what we are justifiably sure of is false.
> We are justifiably sure that p.
> Therefore, p may be false.

If this argument works for some value of p, it works for every value, in which case scepticism is vindicated. But the argument fails to work for the same reason that the Bacon argument fails. Given the second premise, there is good independent evidence that bears on whether p is false, and therefore the frequency information in the first premise is of no value.

Nor does it help to replace the argument by

> Sometimes what we think we are justifiably sure of is false.
> We think we are justifiably sure that p.
> Therefore, p may be false.

Although the second premise no longer implies that there is good independent evidence as to whether p is false, there still *is* such evidence. If the sceptic wants to deny this, then he needs a further argument, which is to say that the frequency argument for scepticism fails unless a different one works. Thus we can retain the frequency argument for toleration without endorsing an analogous argument for scepticism.

2. FALLIBILISM

Toleration involves embracing a kind of fallibilism, since toleration involves conceding the widespread possibility that there is evidence of an error-disclosing sort. Yet philosophers who deserve the name "fallibilists" often fail to mark relevant distinctions with sufficient care. As a result, they end up either disclaiming absolute certainty or at least failing to establish that we are often justified in claiming absolute certainty, in the sense defined in chapter 3, section 2. But let us consider some characteristic views, to ensure that a tolerant form of fallibilism can indeed avoid a binding commitment to scepticism.[4]

James draws a promising distinction between an *absolutist* and an *empiricist* conception of knowledge:

> The absolutists in this matter say that we not only can attain to knowing truth, but we can *know when* we have attained to knowing it; while the empiricists think that although we may attain it, we cannot infallibly know when. To *know* is one thing, and to know for certain *that* we know is another.

On the face of it this is very close to the distinction between a tolerant knowledge claim, which avoids claiming higher-order knowledge, and a dogmatic knowledge claim, which claims higher-order knowledge. Yet James characterizes empiricistic knowledge in a way that makes it less demanding than knowledge in the present ideal sense. He divorces an empiricist claim from an appeal to objective evidence, which in turn divorces it from implying anything about the absolutely total evidence and hence divorces it from a certainty claim. Thus, he says that when an empiricist holds something to be true he simply means that "the total drift of thinking continues to confirm it," which implies that an empiricistic claim does not try to predict the results of future inquiry.[5]

James aligns empiricist knowledge with something less than knowledge in the present ideal sense, on the assumption that anything more demanding must be knowledge of an absolutist sort. If he is right, toleration would have to involve disclaiming knowledge in the present sense, since it involves disclaiming absolutist knowledge. But this is a false dichotomy. We can continue to claim knowledge in a sense that involves being absolutely sure of what we know without having to be sure that we know it. The absolute certainty of what we know does not require the absolute certainty of our knowing it. Consequently, we can exercise toleration by not being sure whether we have knowledge, while avoiding scepticism by being sure of what we know. We can reject the absolutist position while refusing to become empiricistic.

Peirce similarly operates with an oversimplified dichotomy when he contrasts a scientific approach with a search for absolute certainty:

> The scientific spirit requires a man to be at all times ready to dump his whole cartload of beliefs, the moment experience is against them. The desire to learn forbids him to be perfectly cocksure that he knows already. Besides positive science can only rest on experience; and experience can never result in absolute certainty, exactitude, necessity, or universality.[6]

Peirce is right to commend a readiness to dump one's beliefs and to condemn being cocksure that one already has knowledge. But we can endorse this kind of tolerant fallibilism without disclaiming absolute certainty or epistemic necessity. We don't have to be cocksure that we know that Moscow is in Russia in order to be justifiably sure that it is.

Peirce's argument against fixed beliefs supports a need for toleration but fails to establish scepticism. He draws on the premise that our most cherished beliefs are often rejected by others in such a way that there is no reason for preferring ours over theirs. But, although our cherished beliefs are often opposed, they are only occasionally opposed in a way that destroys our justification for being sure of them. In some cases opposition is not voiced by peers. And even if a peer argues vigorously against what we claim to know, we can continue to be justifiably sure if his arguments have counterintuitive elements. Consequently, the facts merely establish that, for any given belief, there *may* be a justification-defeating objection. They do not establish that there will be one. Thus, whereas they do support a tolerant fallibilism, they fail to support scepticism.

Fallibilists often appeal to the fact that given methods are error-prone.[7] But this appeal adds nothing new in principle. It merely establishes that, no matter how careful, detached, thorough, public, or repetitive our procedures have been, our conclusions may always be undermined by further considerations. It does not establish that our conclusions may be false. This is because there is no independent evidence concerning what the results of further inquiry will be, whereas there is independent evidence concerning whether our conclusions are false, viz., the evidence afforded by adopting the given procedures. Consequently, the frequency argument is legitimate in the one case and not in the other.

Divorcing fallibilism from scepticism clearly involves preserving the view that even an ideal knower need not know that he knows. The source of this view is that someone can be justifiably sure of something without having to be justifiably sure that there is no good counterevidence. His justifiably believing in the absence of such evidence is enough. He must be sure of what he knows, but he need not be sure about the evidence that justifies his being sure.

Hilpinen disagrees. He thinks that if one's evidence is adequate for knowledge, it must also be adequate for knowing that one knows. He thinks that "Complete evidence must . . . terminate the inquiry concerning p . . . no further inquiry (that is, no additional factual information) is needed to ensure that the evidence is, indeed, complete."[8] But evidence can terminate an inquiry concerning p without terminating an inquiry concerning the completeness of the evidence. We can reach a point where we are entitled to judge that p is certain without yet being entitled to judge that it is certain that p is certain. Granted, we must be able to determine that the evidence is complete, in the sense that we must be justified in believing that there is no good counterevidence. But this does not require us to be justifiably sure that there is no such evidence.

Hintikka thinks that at least conclusive knowledge must be iterative, if by "conclusive knowledge" we mean knowledge that excludes the possibility of refutation.[9] This much is correct. But it does not establish that knowledge in the present ideal sense is iterative, since there is no reason to think that such knowledge is conclusive. Thus Hintikka fails to establish that knowledge must be iterative if the claiming of such knowledge involves claiming the epistemic necessity of what is known. Even this type of knowledge need not be conclusive in the indicated sense. Consequently, a fallibilist can disclaim conclusive knowledge in Hintikka's sense without on that account becoming a sceptic. He can claim both the absolute certainty of things and the epistemic necessity of things.

3. BETWEEN DOGMATISM AND SCEPTICISM

We have seen that arguments for toleration do not favour scepticism and that, similarly, a healthy fallibilism need not lead to scepticism. Some will probably disagree, however, since they feel strongly that an aversion to dogmatism is a legitimate motive for scepticism. Is such a feeling supported by reasons that have not already been answered?

If we undogmatically keep open the possibility of good counterevidence, and if we also concede that there are many ways in which, and many occasions on which, such counterevidence may emerge, a sceptic might argue that, simply by the law of averages, one of these possibilities is eventually bound to be realized. If so, there is probably good counterevidence in virtually every given case and virtually nothing is certain.[10] But the law of averages cannot be used in this way. A possibility becomes a long-run probability only if the given evidence indicates nothing more specific than that the possibility is one of a number of alternative possibilities at each stage in the run; e.g., getting the queen of hearts is probable in a long run of independent draws only if evidence indicates indifferently that the queen is one card in the deck. But the possibility of good counterevidence is not established by evidence that indicates indifferently that one of several possible pieces of evidence at each stage in a run is good counterevidence. Rather, it is established by the frequency of unexpected refutations in like cases. Consequently, the proper analogy is with a situation where only a few decks similar to our deck have contained the queen of hearts. We cannot on this evidence say that getting the queen from our deck is a long-run probability. For any number of draws, getting the queen remains a mere possibility. Similarly, for any length of run, good counterevidence remains a mere possibility and certainty is preserved.

Harman suggests that claiming knowledge, in a sense that requires a knower to be permanently justified in being sure, might lead to dogmatism in the following way:

> If I know that h is true, I know that any evidence against h is evidence against something that is true; so I know that such evidence is misleading. But I should disregard what I know is misleading. So, once I know that h is true, I am in a position to disregard any future evidence that seems to tell against h.

Harman's reply to the argument is to soften the demands on knowledge.[11] But there is another way. As a knower I do know that any counterevidence is against something true. But I do not thereby know that any additional counterevidence will be discredited by further evidence. Hence I do not know that any such evidence will be misleading in that sense. Consequently, I need not disregard future counterevidence, since it may not be misleading, in which case I need not be dogmatic. I can therefore avoid dogmatism while still claiming ideal knowledge.

Rejecting dogmatism is consistent with claiming knowledge only if a knowledge claimant can concede the possibility that what he knows is certain to be false. This is sound only if "It may be that it is certain that p" does not entail "It is certain that p," which seems legitimate, since a concession of the form "It may be that s" seems not to entail s. In short, using "M" for epistemic possibility, we have the rule

$$(s) \quad Ms \nrightarrow s$$

And using "N" for epistemic necessity, we have the substitution instance

$MNp \nrightarrow Np$

Hacking, however, favours the following counterinstance to the rule:

$MM \sim p \rightarrow M \sim p$

He thinks that any inquiry that establishes p must prove that $M \sim p$ is false, which for him underwrites

$\sim M \sim p \rightarrow \sim MM \sim p$

and by contraposition yields the counterinstance.[12] But why should we agree that establishing p involves more than proving its negation false? It does involve claiming that it is impossible for p to be false. But this does not involve claiming that the possible falsity of p is also impossible. I can claim that it is impossible for "London is on the Thames" to be false and still sensibly investigate whether this claim is correct. Hence I can concede the possibility that the proposition's falsity is not really impossible—a possibility that would be realized if good counterevidence did turn up. Thus the counterinstance fails and the rule stands. We can undogmatically concede the possibility of a complete refutation of what we know.

Lehrer tries to link dogmatism with a claim to know something for certain, by working on the condition that such knowledge must exclude all chance of error.[13] But to hold that knowledge excludes any chance of error about what is known, in the sense that it excludes any chance that the proposition which happens to be known is false, is not to share a dogmatist's conviction that we have such knowledge. We can reject scepticism by holding that we do have knowledge, and yet also reject dogmatism by conceding the chance that we do not have it. In other words, we can adopt a position like that of a juror in a murder trial who accepts a guilty verdict, and with it the claim that the accused certainly committed the murder, and yet has sincere reservations about whether the verdict is correct in view of the evidence.

Insensitivity to the distinction between the possibility of good counterevidence and the possibility that a proposition is false leads Popper to reject both dogmatism and certainty. He thinks that, no matter how strong our argument seems, an ingenious thinker may always detect loopholes in it.[14] But the possibility of loophole detection need only be the possibility that good grounds for doubt will be uncovered, which is not the same as the possibility that the theory is false. The latter possibility requires that there *be* some good counterevidence, not merely that some be possible. Hence we can accept the possibility of a loophole, deny that there actually is one, and in that way reject dogmatism without rejecting certainty.

Lakatos ignores the same distinction when he portrays dogmatism and scepticism as exhaustive options in philosophy of mathematics.[15] He rightly insists, against dogmatism, that counterxamples are always possible. But he wrongly assumes, with scepticism, that it automatically follows that we can never justifiably deny the existence of counterexamples for a given proposition. If our intuitions are strong, our inquiry thorough, our background adequate to the material's complexity, and our results widely endorsed by experts, we can justifiably claim the absence of counterexamples while conceding their possibility. Granted, at mathematically sophisticated levels such conditions may be hard to satisfy. But at least they can be satisfied at elementary levels, which is enough to establish the absence of philosophical, as distinct from mathematical, grounds for doubt. Hence there is a middle way. We can preserve some certainty in mathematics without becoming dogmatic.

Unger offers three argments to connect being sure with being dogmatic. If he is right, being undogmatic involves being unsure and hence involves scepticism. First, he argues that refusing to accept any counterevidence as good is just as dogmatic as refusing to countenance the possibility of counterevidence. Second, he argues that being sure involves holding a strong belief, where strength is measured by one's unwillingness to accept difficulties as genuine. Third, he argues that being sure is a limit that is best understood as either a complete unwillingness to consider the relevance of new evidence or a complete willingness to risk everything if betting.[16]

The first argument rightly calls both attitudes "dogmatic" but wrongly assumes that being sure must involve one of them. Someone can deny that there is good counterevidence and on that account be sure, while conceding both the possibility of counterevidence and the possibility that it is worth something. Unger tries to eliminate this contingency by arguing that anyone who concedes that he would not be sure that $1 + 1 = 2$ if a respected authority denied it is not really sure of the equation now. Concerning the particular instance, Unger is right. Being prepared to be unsure the moment an authority disagreed probably indicates some present unsureness. But if large numbers of authorities disagreed, and if they offered impressive disproofs, and if one's intuitions started to cloud, being prepared to be unsure in those circumstances does not reveal a current unsureness. Consequently, someone can undogmatically concede the appropriate possibilities without betraying a lack of sureness.

The second argument offers an unnecessary, and unsuitable, measure of a belief's strength. Strength in this context is a matter of whether someone finds something absolutely certain. If he does, then his belief has the required strength and he is sure. Having such strength does not involve taking difficulties lightly. On the contrary, it involves attending seriously to whether proposed difficulties will upset the certainty judgment. Hence it does not involve dogmatism.

The third argument rightly views being sure as a limit. But the limit stems from the judgment that there is no good counterevidence in the absolutely total evidence. No judgment can go any farther in this particular direction. Yet someone who reaches this limit can still be willing to consider new evidence in case it undermines the judgment, and he can refuse to bet everything in case the judgment turns out wrong. Consequently, someone can be sure without being dogmatic, and Unger's arguments fail to show that scepticism is the only alternative to dogmatism.

4. OTHER SCEPTICAL ARGUMENTS

The distinctions that have helped us divorce toleration from scepticism can also help us respond nondogmatically to other familiar sceptical arguments, notably the verification argument and the dream argument.

THE VERIFICATION ARGUMENT

Malcolm detects the following sceptical argument in Lewis and some logical positivists:

> For any empirical proposition, p, there are specifiable circumstances, c, such that were any c circumstances to obtain *ceteris paribus*, p would not be certain.
>
> It is not certain that no c circumstances will obtain *ceteris paribus*.
>
> Therefore, p is not certain.[17]

Malcolm thinks that the argument is valid and that the first premise is true. Since he does not think that empirical propositions are uncertain, he therefore attacks the second premise, which forces him to claim that it is certain that no c circumstances will obtain. This is in effect to claim that good counterevidence is impossible and hence is a form of dogmatism. For example, he concedes that if I suddenly felt no hands in the next few seconds in a suitable setting, it would not be certain that I now have hands. Hence he is forced to assert, dogmatically, that it is impossible for me thus to feel no hands.

The first premise is sound. But we can avoid a dogmatic rejection of the second premise by rejecting the argument's validity. Accepting the second premise merely implies the possibility of a c circumstance's obtaining, not its actually obtaining. On the other hand, accepting the first premise merely implies that p is uncertain if a c circumstance actually obtains, not if one is simply possible. Thus, the two premises do not jointly imply p's uncertainty. Instead, they imply the possibility that p is uncertain, which is a tolerant conclusion and not scepticism. This confirms the general principle that only tolerant conclusions can be extracted from tolerant premises.

The Dream Argument

Can we answer the dream argument without having to resort to a dogmatic Cartesian theology, or to some atheological surrogate? A dream sceptic holds that since I may be dreaming right now, many of my beliefs may be false, in which case I have very little knowledge in the ideal sense. He does not have to say that I *am* dreaming now, only that I *may* be dreaming. Hence, whatever else we say, we cannot reply that in implying that he is dreaming he undermines the very basis of his doubts. He only implies that he may be dreaming, which allows him to assume that he probably is not.[18]

The hypothesis that I am currently dreaming does seem to be unverifiable. For one thing, verification seems to involve consciousness and hence to be impossible in a dream. For another, any evidence that I might have in a dream would probably be discredited by the fact that it is in a dream. Finally, if I am dreaming now, it is probably impossible to distinguish it from a waking state and hence to verify that it is a dream. Nevertheless, this does not make the hypothesis unintelligible or my currently being in a dream impossible. It only means that I may now be in a state such that if I am in it, I cannot possibly tell that I am, which is not an absurd result.

One thing we can say at the outset is that in this instance the sceptic has the burden of proof. I find it intuitively plausible that I am awake and not dreaming. The sceptic therefore has to convince me that my intuition is mistaken or unreliable. Moreover, in saying that I may be currently dreaming, the sceptic makes an epistemic modal claim that needs some kind of support. Epistemic possibilities do not just emerge from thin air. True, claiming something's possibility is not to claim very much. But it does require some supporting considerations, however slight.

One sceptical argument appeals to the logical possibility of my now being in a dream. For instance, Moore comes very close to endorsing a logical ground for dream scepticism. He concedes that, if it is logically possible that all my present experiences and memories should be in a dream, it follows that I may now be dreaming. He then tries to avoid the sceptical conclusion by rejecting the logical possibility.[19] This is not a happy solution, especially since he allows the logical possibility that all my present experiences (excluding my memories) should be in a dream while refusing to conclude from this that I may now be dreaming. He is generally reluctant to move from a premise about logical possibility to a conclusion about epistemic possibility, and rightly so. The fact that a conjunction with two conjuncts is logically consistent does not mean that, given the truth of the first conjunct, the second one may be true. For example, the consistency of "I exist, and I'm not currently thinking about philosophy" does not mean that, given that I exist, I may not be currently thinking about philosophy. Hence the consistency of "e, and I am now dreaming," where e describes all my present experiences and memories, does not mean that I may be dreaming now. The dream sceptic needs a better ground than this.

He might therefore try an empirical premise, arguing that I may now be dreaming because realistic dreams have occurred. Malcolm develops an interesting reply to this argument, insisting on a systematic ambiguity between dream descriptions and descriptions of waking states. If he is right, the empirical dream argument is probably no better than the argument that, since (bridal) showers have been cancelled without notice, a given (rain) shower may be so cancelled.[20]

The ambiguity thesis is not entirely convincing, however, in spite of Malcolm's efforts to support it. He argues that it no more follows from someone's thinking in a dream that he is thinking than it follows from his mountain climbing in a dream that he is mountain climbing. And he argues that a dream report conclusively fixes the contents of a dream, whereas the report of a waking state can be corrected. His first argument is suspect because, whereas "He climbed a mountain in a dream" just means "He dreamt that he climbed a mountain," "He thought of the solution in a dream" does not just mean "He dreamt that he thought of the solution"—he needn't have dreamt any such thing. The second argument is also unconvincing. External evidence can have a bearing on the accuracy of dream reports in much the same way that it can have a bearing on the accuracy of after-image reports (see chapter 7, section 5).

Still, this does not mean that the empirical argument succeeds. It fails to work because it is an illegitimate frequency argument. It moves from a premise about the incidence of realistic dreams to the conclusion that I may currently be dreaming, where there is independent reason to say that I am not dreaming. For instance, my wife just assured me that I am not dreaming, which means that there is good authoritative evidence against the dream hypothesis.

Yet if the empirical argument is so bad, why does it hold any attraction? It has a veneer of plausibility because it is so easily confused with a good frequency argument. We can legitimately argue that, given that there are realistic dreams, events may occur that indicate that I am in fact dreaming right now. For instance, I may subsequently experience awakening and remembering having dreamt all this, and others may assure me that I have been asleep all along. This argument works because there is no independent evidence as to whether such considerations will occur, aside from the evidence concerning the incidence of realistic dreams. But this argument only establishes that there may be good evidence that I am now dreaming. It does not establish that I may be dreaming. It helps to oppose a dogmatic claim to know that I am awake and not dreaming. But it does not support scepticism.[21]

5. SUMMARY

A variety of antidogmatic considerations are sound, but they all fail to generate scepticism. There *is* a middle way. It consists in making undogmatic knowledge claims, where "knowledge" is deliberately used in its ideal sense. This means that we can be sure of many things while rarely, if ever, being sure that we know such things. Such a position of tolerant gnosticism works because considerations that prevent us from being justifiably sure that we have knowledge fail to prevent us from being justifiably sure of what we know. To gain a better understanding of this point, however, we need to consider more carefully the nature of justification.

CHAPTER NINE

Justification

1. INTRODUCTION

I have reserved an analysis of justification until this point because the analytic task is hard to separate from a treatment of sceptical issues. Some philosophers have serious doubts about whether our conclusions can ever be justified. Some are particularly concerned about the justification of nondeductive conclusions. Others would include deduction as well. Any such doubts apply to whether we have knowledge in the ideal sense.

I shall eventually concentrate on nondeductive conclusions, using enumerative induction as a test case. But first let us examine the general conditions of being justifiably sure of something, regardless of whether we are sure because of an inference or by virtue of an intuition.

The type of justification to be described is normally called *epistemic* and is distinct from justification in moral, legal, or prudential senses. For example, someone can be morally justified in lying, legally justified in character assassination, or prudentially justified in being confident, without having a corresponding epistemic justification. In the present context the word "justification" is reserved strictly for epistemic justification.

2. CONDITIONS OF JUSTIFICATION

Let us say that we are justifiably sure of something provided we satisfy four conditions:

(i) We find it plausible, or at least we would have found it plausible had we been governed by rational motives.

(ii) It is accordingly plausible.

(iii) We have no counterevidence, unless either it is discredited by our remaining evidence or, given the nature of our meta evidence, it probably is discredited by further evidence.

> (iv) Given the nature of our meta evidence, there probably is
> no additional counterevidence that is any good.

The counterfactual option in (i) is included because of the technical use of "being sure" in the analysandum. For instance, a self-deceiver can be justifiably sure of something even though he does not find it plausible, provided he would have found it plausible had he been governed by rational considerations.

The term "accordingly" in (ii) refers back to (i). The condition implies, for example, that if we find a belief plausible because of what we observe, our observing what we do must be plausible and this must yield the belief's plausibility.

The probability in (iii) and (iv) is merely relative probability. Our relevant evidence can be classified in such a way that, relative to our meta evidence, evidence of that kind probably has a favourable track record. Thus, even if we have counterevidence that our evidence does not itself discredit, our evidence can still probably be of a kind that is usually augmented by discrediting evidence. Similarly, our evidence can probably be of a kind that is usually not augmented by good counterevidence. In that case, relative to our meta evidence, our evidence probably contains no good counterevidence and there probably is no further counterevidence that is any good.

The meta evidence that indicates the probable reliability of our relevant evidence consists in our remembering that evidence of that kind has generally stood up well in the face of proposed difficulties, while not having further evidence that discredits or outweighs this memory. Such meta evidence indicates that our evidence is probably of a kind that has performed well in the past. It thereby establishes the plausibility of thinking that our evidence is of a kind that performs well at any time. Thus if we have no further evidence to the contrary, our meta evidence establishes that our relevant evidence is probably of a reliable kind, which in turn establishes that in the particular case at hand there probably is no good counterevidence.

This means that we can tell when we satisfy conditions of being justifiably sure of something. We can tell intuitively whether we find something plausible, whether we possess any good counterevidence, and whether we have the type of meta evidence that indicates the probable reliability of our relevant evidence. Indeed, we can even know intuitively that we are justified, provided our intuitions are correct and reliable. This does not mean that we can know that we have knowledge, however, since it still does not mean that we can know that what we are justifiably sure of is in fact certain. Knowing that we are justifiably sure allows us to say that, relative to our evidence, there probably is no good counterevidence. It does not allow us to say that there certainly is none.

In fact, this is why we can claim to satisfy the conditions of being justifiably sure of something without generating an infinite regress. When we claim that there probably is no good counterevidence, we only make a relative claim on our meta evidence. We do not even claim absolute probability, much less absolute certainty. As a result, we do not imply that there is no further good contrary meta evidence. We merely imply that we don't have any. For example, if I claim to be justifiably sure that I have two hands, I simply imply that I *have* no meta evidence that faults my memory that the type of evidence I have for saying that I have two hands has generally performed well when confronted by new evidence. I do not imply that there *is* no such meta evidence.

Now, since a claim to be justifiably sure of something implies a relative-probability claim about the remaining evidence, those who distrust basing acceptance on relative probability might argue that we then cannot accept a claim that we are justified in being sure, which would be an odd result. But, as we saw in chapter 2, section 6, if in a given situation relative probability is all we can get, we *can* legitimately use it as a guide to rational belief. And in this case nothing more is available if we are to avoid generating an infinite regress.

We can thus cease to be justifiably sure of something in two ways. First, we can acquire counterevidence that is neither discredited by our evidence nor probably discredited by further evidence. Second, we can acquire meta evidence that either leads us to abandon the memory of reliability or discredits the memory. For example, we might come to realize that our procedures are not as thorough as we originally thought, which leads us to revise our memory about their reliability. Or we might learn that our memory is based largely on poor authority.

Identifying a reliable kind of evidence is strictly an empirical matter. There is no kind such that, necessarily, evidence of that kind is always, or even generally, insulated against subsequent refutation. All we can do is identify contingent marks of reliability—e.g., features like thoroughness, detachment, successful repetition, ample support, intelligence in organization, rigour in testing, and intersubjective agreement. Moreover, change is quite possible. For instance, a calculating procedure might be probably reliable relative to fairly unsophisticated meta evidence and then be probably unreliable relative to meta evidence that incorporates the results of mechanical calculations. Of course, conceding the empirical nature of reliability judgments will not satisfy someone who assumes that justification must be governed entirely by universal *a priori* principles. But this is a wrongheaded, and dangerous, assumption—wrongheaded because such principles are unnecessary, dangerous because it can lead to the conclusion that justification is impossible.

Given the foregoing explanation of the conditions of justification, we can now say, elliptically, that we are justifiably sure of something if, and only if, (i) we find it plausible, (ii) it is plausible, (iii) we have no good counterevidence, and (iv) our evidence is probably reliable.

3. SUBJECTIVITY

Justification is subjective, in the sense that it depends on whether we find, or, in suitable circumstances would have found, something plausible, and whether the absence of good counterevidence is probable relative to our meta evidence. Justification is not purely subjective, however, since it depends on whether what we take to be plausible *is* plausible, and on whether any of our evidence *is* good counterevidence, and also because even relative probability is not purely subjective (see chapter 2, section 2).

This means that, contrary to some accounts, justification is not simply a matter of what we believe. For instance, Lehrer holds, roughly, that we justifiably believe something if, and only if, as impartial truth-seekers we believe that the proposition has a better chance of being true than any competing belief.[1] This innocently implies that we can be justifiably sure of something provided we believe that no competing belief has any chance of being true. Yet it also harmfully implies that one person can be justifiably sure of something and another person can be justifiably unsure of it, even though they possess the same evidence—e.g., that I as a nonsceptic can be justifiably sure of many things, whereas Lehrer as a sceptic can be justifiably unsure of them, even though we are familiar with the same philosophical arguments. Now, both positions are equally responsible. But only one of them is justified by our common evidence. The question

"Which one?" is to be decided by determining whether our evidence contains good grounds for doubting everything. It may contain such grounds. Hence Lehrer's position may be the justified one, in which case mine is not. Or the contrary may be the case. But they cannot both be justified. The claim that a given competing position is justified is not simply an external claim about what someone believes to be the case. It implies an appraisal of the given evidence, which gets us involved in the substantive issue itself. Thus, we can preserve a more ideal notion of justification, and hence of knowledge, by not formulating justification in terms of what we believe.[2]

4. INDUCTION

The above account can be used to eliminate many of the problems that philosophers are apt to raise against justified inference. To see this, let us take enumerative induction as a test case, since classically many of the complaints tend to focus on it.

Hume thinks that "even after the observation of the frequent or constant conjunction of objects, we have no reason to draw any inference concerning any object beyond those of which we have had experience."[3] He is right if he means that merely observing constant conjunction does not justify concluding that unobserved objects will exhibit the same constancy. But he also thinks that nothing can be added to our observations to justify a general conclusion. He argues, rightly, that no *a priori* principle, such as "Nature is uniform," can be found to close the gap. And he rightly thinks that if we try to close the gap with an empirical generalization, we face the same theoretical problem when we try to justify its acceptance. If these exhaust the available options, justified conclusions are beyond us, regardless of whether we are sure of them or merely find them probable.

Fortunately, justification does not require a general principle, either *a priori* or empirical, to close Hume's gap. It requires the addition of two conditions that are within our grasp and that are not question-begging. The conditions are, first, that we have no good counterevidence, and, second, that our observations are embedded in a kind of evidence that is probably reliable. The first condition is simply a matter for intuition. We can find it intuitively plausible that we have no good counterevidence with respect to a given conclusion. The probable reliability in the second condition is relative to our meta evidence. It is a matter of our remembering that the given kind of evidence has been reliable, while not having any preponderant reason to discredit our memory as a basis for concluding that such evidence is always reliable. And that we have such an unfettered memory is also a matter for intuition. Thus, we can ascertain that both conditions are satisfied without having to draw on any *a priori* principles or any conclusions of the sort under investigation.

To see how this works in a specific instance, consider the conclusion that all men are mortal. We are justifiably sure of this conclusion if we satisfy four conditions:

(1) We find it plausible that all men are mortal because we observe men dying.

(2) It is plausible that all men are mortal because it is plausible that we observe men dying.

(3) We do not have any good counterevidence with respect to whether all men are mortal.

(4) Given our meta evidence, our evidence with respect to whether all men are mortal is probably reliable.

We can establish that each of these conditions is satisfied either by intuition or by deducing it from intuitive premises.

Condition (4) is apt to arouse the most controversy, since in saying that our relevant evidence is probably reliable, we are drawing a conclusion from what we remember, viz., that such evidence has been reliable. And this can seem to be a question-begging step. But it is not in fact an inductive inference. It is a complex *a priori* probabilistic step of the following type:

(a) We remember that most A's have been $\varnothing$.

(b) Therefore, it is plausible that most A's have been $\varnothing$.

(c) Therefore, it is plausible that most A's are $\varnothing$.

(d) We have no preponderant counterevidence in this respect.

(e) Therefore, relative to our evidence it is probable that most A's are $\varnothing$.

The steps to (b), (c), and (e) are in each case deductive, and (a) and (d) can both be intuitively plausible. Thus, we can establish the probable reliability of our evidence for human mortality without having to draw on an *a priori* principle of the uniformity of nature and without having to take a prior inductive step. The only things we need are *a priori plausibility* principles that sanction the steps to (b) and to (c).

Popper argues that condition (3) fails to be satisfied and suggests that, if the conditions of justification fail to apply here, they cannot be reasonably expected to apply in any instance. His proposed counterevidence is, e.g., that bacteria are not bound to die.[4] But this by itself does not work against *human* mortality or the observations that support it. Granted, further biomedical experimentation may disclose a link and provide evidence that supports at least the possibility of human survival. But this simply means that we may someday have good counterevidence, not that we do have it now. Consequently, nothing introduced by Popper forces me to revise my intuitive assessment of our relevant evidence. And even if it did, I should not on that account concede that justificatory conditions are never satisfied in other instances—e.g., in the case of conclusions like "Cats never grow on trees" and "Human beings need oxygen in order to survive." Moreover, as long as objections to a particular conclusion are simply empirical arguments against a counterpart of condition (3), they are not sceptical objections in the technical sense of philosophical objections—that is, they fail to show that the conditions of justification are somehow in principle unsatisfiable.

Another empirical objection is to insist that, for most inductive conclusions, drawn in the kind of setting that characterizes the conclusion that all men are mortal, a refutation has in fact subsequently occurred. This is a sufficiently general objection to be philosophical and hence is relevantly sceptical. But as far as I can tell, what it says is false. Inductive evidence of the relevant kind has usually not been augmented by good counterevidence. Granted, it sometimes has, even in scientific contexts where generalizations have been adopted with great care and circumspection. But unless more than half are refuted, the frequency argument still establishes that the conclusion that all men are mortal probably will not be refuted. Moreover, even if most relevant universal conclusions have turned out to be refuted, this by itself would not destroy our justification for drawing empirical conclusions that are not quite so universal, e.g. as in "Men in our type of environment are all mortal", "Smoking is a health hazard," or "Water normally boils at 100°C." Our evidence may not be reliable enough to justify unqualified universal conclusions. But it can still justify many conclusions of a sort that we do frequently draw.

Duhem's comment that "the physicist is never sure he has exhausted all the imaginable" competing explanations can be applied to inductive conclusions.[5] Although "All men are mortal" does account for our observations of dying men, so does "All men are mortal except for the prime minister." And, although we can eventually extend our observations to exclude the latter explanation, further competitors of this sort are always available. As a result, Duhem's comment suggests that we cannot transform an inductive conclusion into an indisputable truth. Indeed, preferring the generalization over its remaining unrefuted competitors may then be so arbitrary that it is not at all justified, not even as a probabilistic conclusion.

But if the generalization does perform well through a sequence of tests, in the sense that the results of crucial experiments favour it over selected competitors, this creates the plausibility that it will withstand further competition. And if initially promising competitors have been vanquished, if the tests have been rigorous, and if peer criticism has been honestly sought, we can predict that the generalization will probably survive future competition. In short, we can assemble meta evidence that justifies the claim that there is probably no good counterevidence, in which case we can be justifiably sure of the generalization. Granted, as Duhem suggests, a successful competitor is always possible, since we cannot enumerate completely the various hypotheses that *may* cover a given set of observations. But this simply means that some competitor may survive further testing instead of the generalization, which in turn simply means that good counterevidence is possible. It does not mean that there *will* be good counterevidence. Hence our justification for predicting the absence of good counterevidence remains, and with it our justification for being sure of the generalization.

Goodman's "new riddle of induction" raises a special difficulty in connection with competing explanations. But I shall defer treatment of this problem until we look at various puzzles concerning confirmation in the next chapter.

This defence of the justification of inductive conclusions does imply that, in a sense, inductive rules are unavailable. For example, suppose that we say

> If we observe a large number of A's to be B's, and we have no good counterevidence, and our observations are made in highly varied circumstances, then we are justified in concluding that all A's are B's.

Now, if the condition that our observations are highly varied simply *means* that they are of a technically reliable sort, the above sentence merely asserts the formal conditions of a conclusion's being justified. To that extent it is not a rule for regulating our conclusions in order to get them to satisfy justificatory conditions. On the other hand, if the link between highly varied observations and reliable observations is not just analytic, it must be empirical. In that case we do not have an *a priori* rule but an empirical guideline. In this sense, then, there are no inductive rules.[6] But this does not mean that there are no specifiable conditions of being justified, or that we cannot satisfy such conditions in the case of drawing inductive conclusions.

5. ALTERNATIVE ACCOUNTS

The distinctive features of the present account will come into sharper focus if we compare it briefly with some familiar responses to Hume's scepticism.

THE PROBABILISTIC ANSWER

According to Russell, we can draw probabilistic conclusions on the basis of observing exclusively positive instances, where the degree of probability increases with an increase in the number of observations.[7] But the probability he has in mind is strictly relative, which means that he fails to account for the justification of absolute epistemic claims, even probabilistic ones.

In this connection, we must keep firmly in mind the distinction between the conclusion drawn (say, that all men are mortal) and the claim that this conclusion is certain. The certainty claim implies that there is no good counterevidence and, as we have seen, whether this implicit judgment is sound is a matter of relative probability on our meta evidence. But that simply means that the legitimacy of the certainty claim is itself partly a matter of relative probability. It does not mean that the certainty claim is relative or, therefore, that the conclusion is only relatively probable. In other words, whereas we are saying "It is only probable, relative to our meta evidence, that men are certainly all mortal," we are not just saying "Relative to our evidence it is probable that all men are mortal." That is why Russell's proposal falls short.

THE ANALYTIC ANSWER

Strawson holds it to be analytically true "that, other things being equal, the evidence for a generalization is strong in proportion as the number of favourable instances, and the variety of circumstances in which they have been found, is great."[8] But a universe *is* possible in which large numbers of exclusively favourable and highly varied observations are usually followed by good counterevidence, in which case such observations would not provide strong evidence in support of a generalization. Thus, as it stands the connection is not analytic. Moreover, if Strawson simply makes it analytic by resolving to use the expression "numerous and varied observations" to mean "observations that provide strong evidence," he still has to establish against Hume that we do make numerous and varied observations in *that* sense. This requires making an empirical assertion about the performance to date of inductive inferences. Appealing to analyticity is therefore wrong or incomplete.

The same comment holds against Barker's claim that "it is inconceivable that inductive inferences should not *probably* be the most successful kind in the long run."[9] It is quite conceivable that, over a long run, inductive inferences do in fact break down, in the sense that good counterevidence subsequently turns up more often than not. It would then be improbable that they will generally stand up in the future. What we cannot say, logically, is that inductive inferences have managed to do as well as they in fact have done *and* that they will probably not be generally successful in the future. This conjunction *is* inconceivable. But its first conjunct concerns only an empirical fact, not an analytic truth.

PRAGMATIC VINDICATION

Salmon, following Reichenbach, tries to vindicative inductive conclusions pragmatically by arguing that if the adoption of any inference rule will work, adopting an inductive rule will, and that only an inductive rule can avoid contradictions.[10] We have seen that talk of an inductive rule can be misleading. Moreover, even Salmon now has reservations about whether competing rules must all generate contradictions. Finally, a pragmatic approach concedes that there is nothing to choose between expecting some inference rule to work and expecting that none will, which is to concede that no inductive conclusion is justified in the present sense. Consequently, it tries to sidestep Hume's challenge instead of meeting it head-on, which is an unfortunate and unnecessary move.

INDUCTIVE SELF-SUPPORT

Black holds that "when an inductive rule has been reliable (has generated true conclusions from true premises more often than not) in the past, a second-order inductive inference governed by the same rule can show that the rule deserves to be trusted in its next application."[11] This is not quite right as it stands. We *can* say that if our meta evidence indicates that inductive inferences of a specified sort have been reliable in the past, and if we have no strong contrary meta evidence, such inferences will probably be reliable in the future. But this inference only has a relative conclusion. Indeed, its conclusion follows *a priori* from its premises. In this sense, our second-order supporting inference does not have the same structure as the inductive inferences it tries to support. As a result, there is no circularity. In other words, we are not trying to use the conclusion of a specimen of an argument species the merit of which is in question to help defend the merit of that species. Hence we are not using an inductive *self-*supporting argument.

6. DEDUCTION

Deductive inference can seem to create fewer difficulties than induction because, at least in most cases, there is a truth-preserving rule of validity such that if both the premises and the rule are justified, the conclusion must also be justified. There is no such rule in the case of induction.

This does not mean that deductive justificatory problems cannot arise, however. A rule *is* open to challenge and it might seem that there is no possible way to meet such a challenge. Relying on empirical support for an allegedly *a priori* rule looks odd; and, in the case of a fundamental rule like *modus ponens,* trying to defend the rule without at the same time using it seems to be a hopeless venture.[12] But in this case there is no need to accept the task of demonstrating the rule as a condition of justifying its acceptance. *Modus ponens* seems to be intuitively plausible and our intuition seems to be of a reliable sort. Consequently, the question of whether we are justified in accepting *modus ponens* becomes the question of whether these impressions are correct. In other words, in this instance the sceptic has the burden of proof and he will have a difficult time shouldering the burden without presupposing the rule's validity. Moreover, if he does somehow manage to argue in an independent way, it should be equally possible for us to reply in kind. If we succeed, we thereby increase the probability that the intuition will survive criticism, which in turn improves our justification for being sure of the rule. Thus, a defensive justification of a specific deductive inference is possible.

7. SUMMARY

Being justifiably sure of something involves satisfying a mixture of requirements. What we are sure of must be plausible. We cannot possess any good counterevidence. And relative to our meta evidence, our evidence must probably be of a reliable sort. Contrary to Hume, inductive conclusions can satisfy such requirements. Consequently, there is no need to replace absolute inductive conclusions by relative probability claims. On the other hand, we need more than just an analytic connection between specified inductive inferences and reliability. The link must be established empirically. Yet establishing the link does not involve an inductive inference of the sort in question. Hence there is no circularity and no need to abandon justification in favour of a pragmatic vindication.

One group of potential problems remains, however. Justifying a conclusion frequently involves confirmation. If we cannot confirm anything, we cannot discredit counterevidence or establish the reliability of our evidence, in which case justification is beyond us. Let us therefore see whether confirmation is a genuine possibility.

CHAPTER TEN

Confirmation

1. TWO CONCEPTS OF CONFIRMATION

In a weak sense of "confirm" we can confirm something by introducing evidence that adds to its plausibility. For instance, we can add further testimony, or we can confirm a geometrical proposition by observing an example. Let us call this *plausibility-conferring* confirmation.

The sense is weak because such confirmation need not strengthen our case for the hypothesis. One piece of testimony can confirm another piece even if further evidence discredits both pieces. Observing an equal-sided square can confirm 'All squares have equal sides' even though the observation does nothing to improve our case for accepting the general proposition. Accordingly, let us also talk of *evidence-improving* confirmation, where the confirming evidence must outweigh or discredit antecedent counterevidence, or establish or increase the reliability of our evidence.

2. PARADOX

Are there any genuine confirmation paradoxes? That is, do principles that are vital to the possibility of confirmation unavoidably generate absurd results? If they do, confirmation is impossible, in which case justification and knowledge are very likely also impossible.

Four confirmation principles have an attractive veneer:

The observation principle: Observing a $\varnothing x$ confirms "All x's are $\varnothing$."

The consequence principle: Whatever confirms an hypothesis confirms anything entailed by the hypothesis.

> *The equivalence principle:* Whatever confirms an hypothesis confirms any logically equivalent hypothesis.
>
> *The converse consequence principle:* Whatever confirms an hypothesis confirms anything that entails the hypothesis.

Are these principles really indispensable to confirmation, and if so, do they really generate absurdity?

Hempel points out the following apparent paradox.[1] By the observation principle, observing A's that are B's confirms the generalization "All A's are B's." By the equivalence principle, it also confirms the contrapositive "All non-B's are non-A's." By a similar line of reasoning, observing non-B's that are non-A's confirms the generalization by confirming its contrapositive. But then, e.g., observing white swans confirms "All ravens are black," which seems absurd.

If confirmation is simply plausibility-conferring, such a result is not absurd. Observing white swans does confer plausibility on "All ravens are black" via its contrapositive, since it gives us a reason to be more than indifferent toward the generalization. Granted, the reason is highly unreliable because this sort of conclusion is usually subsequently refuted. But that simply means that the confirmation is not evidence-improving. This should come as no surprise, since the observation principle holds only for plausibility-conferring confirmation in any event. That is why observing a positive instance can actually disconfirm a generalization in an evidence-improving sense. For instance, if there is good background evidence that any bird found in Kamloops has differently coloured counterparts in Tahiti, observing a black raven in Kamloops disconfirms "All ravens are black." Thus, the relevant principles do collectively work for plausibility-conferring confirmation but not for evidence-improving confirmation. They will seem to be both essential and absurd only if we neglect this distinction.[2]

Of course, circumstances might be added to a case such that the observation principle works for evidence improvement *in those circumstances,* even when the observation is described solely in negative terms. For example, suppose that there is independent strong support for "All ravens are black" and hence for its contrapositive. Yet suppose that there is some evidence that a nonblack bird in my bathtub is a raven. Observing a solitary white swan in my bathtub in these circumstances, and hence a nonblack nonraven, can provide evidence-improving confirmation for both the contrapositive and the generalization. Thus, in circumstances where the observation does provide evidence-improving confirmation, such confirmation can be effectively transferred via equivalence without any absurdity.

Goodman fears that the principles absurdly imply that every observation confirms every statement. Suppose that by the converse consequence principle, observing q confirms the conjunction $q.r$. By the consequence principle, observing q confirms r, whatever r happens to be. Goodman tries to block such a result by insisting that the observation must "convey credibility to r as well.[3] But on its own this move is ineffective. In the sense in which the observation does confirm the conjunction, it can do so without improving r's status, *provided r* is independently solid. For example, if an army officer predicts that the enemy will attack by sea and at dawn, he can confirm the prediction by adding evidence of an enemy landing-craft deployment, provided there is strong independent evidence of a dawn attack. But that means that r cannot be just any statement. It must either have an independently strong status or itself profit from the observation. Thus paradox is still avoided.

In fact, the consequence principle works only for plausibility-conferring confirmation. An entailing hypothesis can be improved by new evidence when what it entails is not improved, indeed, is even damaged. For example, we can improve the case for p without improving it for $p \vee not\ p$. And we can improve the case for p in a way that actually diminishes the case for $p \vee q$ because it damages the antecedent case for q. These contingencies will seem paradoxical only if we confuse evidence-improving and plausibility-conferring forms of confirmation.[4]

As it stands, the converse consequence principle fails to work at all. It cannot work for plausibility-conferring confirmation, and it needs amending before it can work for evidence-improving confirmation. For example, it implies that confirming p confirms $p.q$, whatever the value of q. But conferring plausibility on p does not confer plausibility on $p.q$. And improving our evidence for p will not improve our evidence for $p.q$ unless further conditions are specified.

Brody therefore offers the following replacement for converse consequence:

> *The explanatory principle:* Whatever confirms an hypothesis confirms anything that explains the hypothesis.[5]

This principle seems solid for plausibility-conferring confirmation. Conferring plausibility on an explanandum does confer plausibility on its explanans. But the principle fails to work for evidence-improving confirmation. For example, suppose that we explain John's behaviour by citing depression and we explain his depression by citing a recent divorce. We can confirm the depression hypothesis by consulting a doctor who also tells us that John's depression is chemically induced and that he is very happy about the divorce. We thereby disconfirm the divorce hypothesis. Thus, further changes in the explanatory principle are needed before it can govern evidence improvement.

We need not dwell on such changes here, however. The present aim is not to undertake a study of confirmation. It is to consider a selection of principles to see whether those that are essential to confirmation also generate absurdity. Enough has been done to indicate that this does not really occur. What happens is that principles that work for plausibility-conferring confirmation appear absurd when they are wrongly taken to govern evidence-improving confirmation. Confirmation therefore harbours no real paradoxes.

3. TESTABILITY

Although there is nothing paradoxical in the nature of evidence improvement, some might still feel that its governing principles underwrite scepticism. For example, Watkins suggests that evidence improvement is a matter of testing, and that degree of confirmation varies directly with the test's severity. Severity is in turn a matter of the antecedent (mathematical) probability of getting a positive result. We thus have this principle:

> *The inverse probability principle:* The lower the antecedent probability of getting a positive result, the higher the degree of confirmation provided by a positive result.[6]

Now, it seems that there is always room for confirming an interesting hypothesis. Consequently, it might seem that we can never be justifiably sure of such an hypothesis, since it might seem that the hypothesis must have a probability less than 1.0 in order that the degree of confirmation can exceed 0.0.

This argument confuses the antecedent probability of getting a positive test result with the antecedent probability of the hypothesis itself. The former must be less than 1.0 if the hypothesis is to be testable, but the latter can be 1.0. For example, suppose that someone convicted of murder is about to tell his parents whether he really did it. If the verdict is justified, he probably will confess, but this probability can be as low as 0.6. In that case the degree of confirmation resulting from a confession would be reasonably high. But the antecedent probability that he committed the murder is still 1.0. Thus, the inverse probability principle is not a disguised source of scepticism.

4. PROJECTION

Goodman introduces a consideration that suggests that inductive conclusions can never be justified.[7] Let "grue" mean "either green and observed before the year 2000 or blue and not observed before then." Suppose that "Emeralds are all green" is an empirical generalization. By the observation principle, the generalization is confirmed by our observing green emeralds. But since all green emeralds observed to date are also grue, those same observations confirm "All emeralds are grue." The observations are of a reliable sort. Hence each generalization satisfies some of the conditions for being justified by our current evidence. Yet since the generalizations cannot both be true, whatever confirms one must by the consequence principle confirm the other's negation. Hence good evidence for one must be good evidence against the other and they cannot both be justified. But from the standpoint of assessing evidence, it seems arbitrary to prefer one over the other. Hence neither is justified.

Since grue-type alternatives can be constructed for virtually any given predicate, this line of reasoning implies that virtually no inductive generalization is justified. It similarly undermines our justification for predictions. Predicting that the first emerald observed after 2000 will be green is then no more justified than predicting it to be blue, which means that neither prediction is justified. To this extent projection would cease to be a rational enterprise.

Goodman thinks that in spite of the foregoing considerations, projecting "green" for emeralds *is* "genuinely confirmed" by our evidence. But instead of defending the view that our evidence justifies the projection, he makes a Humean appeal to custom and general success. Projecting "green" avoids being arbitrary solely insofar as doing so is entrenched in our linguistic and investigative practices. If he is right, we should redefine the concept of knowledge in a way that lets us claim knowledge that emeralds are green without implying that our evidence epistemically justifies the claim. But do we have to concede that epistemic justification is a lost cause?

Merely restricting projection to nontemporal predicates like "green" fails to establish anything in our evidence that inevitably favours such projections.[8] Indeed, circumstances are possible in which projecting a temporal predicate initially seems the better option. For instance, imagine that independent evidence indicates that the very process of observing emeralds currently alters them from blue to green and that a technology to prevent the alteration will be developed in 2000.[9] In that case, projecting "grue" is intuitively more appealing.

Nor does it help to insist that projecting "grue" implies a gratuitous difference between emeralds observed before 2000 and other emeralds. As Goodman points out, if "bleen" means "either blue and observed before 2000 or green and not observed," projecting "green" equally implies a difference, viz., that one group is grue and the other is bleen. Blackburn is unconvinced by this reply. He argues that to view the projection of "grue" as involving equal treatment of emeralds is like saying that a judge who treats all men as *pitchly* is egalitarian, where "pitchly" means "either kindly if rich or unkindly if poor."[10] But uniform pitchly treatment *would* be egalitarian if all poor men were wicked and all rich men were virtuous. Similarly, projecting "grue" instead of "green" might be to treat all emeralds as relevantly the same. This cannot be ruled out *a priori,* in which case projecting "grue" cannot be dismissed on this ground.

Appealing to independent evidence that favours projecting "green" for emeralds is a more promising approach, and yet not quite effective. For example, Jackson thinks that, although emeralds observed to date have all been both green and grue, we independently know that they would have been green and not grue had they remained unobserved. He on this account favours projecting "green." He finds the case analogous to one in which lobsters observed to date have all been red and cooked and we independently know that they would not have been red had they been uncooked. Our independent counterfactual knowledge then discredits our evidence for projecting "red" for lobsters and, he suggests, it similarly discredits our evidence for projecting "grue" for emeralds.[11]

The problem with this particular solution concerns the claim to know independently that, had observed emeralds not been observed, they would have been green and not grue. True, as Jackson points out, knowledge of the counterfactual does not require knowing that unobserved emeralds *are* green, since the counterfactual knowledge is possible even if unobserved emeralds are red. But the counterfactual knowledge must still be based on some sort of evidence. And the question of whether we have evidence that supports a claim to such knowledge is on a par with the question at issue, of whether we have evidence that supports a claim to know that all emeralds are green. Hence we are not entitled to assume that we have the necessary independent knowledge.

Nevertheless, Jackson is right to think that the solution lies in the fact that the given evidence is discredited as evidence for projecting "grue" and not as evidence for projecting "green." He is simply mistaken in identifying the source of the discreditation. There *is* an important difference in the way each projection is related to the supporting evidence. Whereas projecting "green" derives its plausibility from that of "We observe green emeralds," projecting "grue" derives its plausibility from that of "We observe green emeralds and we observe them before 2000." Thus, part of the conjunctive evidence that confers plausibility on projecting "grue" is evidence that confers plausibility on projecting "green" and not conversely. When this happens, and when no independent evidence discredits the evidence for projecting "green," the evidence for projecting "grue" has an asymmetrical dependence on our evidence for projecting "green." Since the latter is not independently discredited, and since the two projections are incompatible, our evidence for projecting "grue" is thereby discredited. Although our evidence does confer plausibility on both projections, and hence it confirms them both in a plausibility-conferring sense, it does not provide good evidence for both, and hence cannot confirm them both in an evidence-improving sense. Observing green emeralds in our circumstances is simply *bad* evidence for concluding that all emeralds are grue. Consequently, we have no good evidence against concluding that they are all green and the conclusion is justified.

The discreditation principle being evoked here is roughly as follows:

The principle of evidential subordination: If evidence *e1* confers plausibility on conclusion *c1*, *e1* contains *e2* as a part, *e2* confers plausibility on *c2, e2* is not independently discredited as evidence for *c2,* and *c1* and *c2* are logically incompatible, then *e1* is bad evidence for *c1.*

Given this principle, our observational evidence for projecting "grue" is bad, whereas our observational evidence for projecting "green" can be good. Similarly, imagine that someone trustworthy says assuringly, "John is a tall fat man, although most fat men are short." His remark is evidence that John is a tall fat man, which in turn is evidence that all fat men are tall. But part of his remark is also evidence that not all fat men are tall. And nothing independently discredits the latter. Consequently, by the subordination principle his remark is bad evidence that all fat men are tall.

The principle allows that in different circumstances our observations could provide, or help to provide, good evidence for projecting "grue," viz. where our evidence for projecting "green" is independently discredited—e. g., where we independently know that observing emeralds now alters them from blue to green, or where we are told on impeccable authority that only observed emeralds are green. But in actual fact there is no such independent discreditation and hence the principle does apply to our evidence for projecting "grue."

The principle also implies that if, in different circumstances, we simply observed "grue" emeralds, without inferring their "grueness" from their "greenness" and the date of our observations, our observations could be good evidence for projecting "grue." This is a commendable result. If our observing "grue" emeralds did acquire such a primitive character, our observational evidence *could* offer worthwhile support for projecting "grue." Whether it did would depend upon what the rest of our evidence was like and in particular on what led us to make such observations. But at least the possibility would be open. Yet again the actual facts are otherwise. We do not just observe "grue" emeralds. Hence our actual evidence for projecting "grue" is bad.

The subordination principle also rules out other "grue"-type options. For example, Skyrms defines "snarf" to mean "either an insect, a ball of wax, a feather, or a mask," and "murkle" to mean "either a green insect, a yellow ball of wax, a purple feather, or a red thing of some other sort." Imagine that there are four objects: one a green insect, one a yellow ball of wax, one a purple feather, and one a mask of unknown colour. The four are all "snarfs," and the first three are "murkle." If we conclude that the fourth "snark" is "murkle," we imply that it is red. Yet we can define concepts that have the same basic structure as "murkle" but that specify a fourth colour other than red; and by parity of reasoning we could then assign any colour to the mask we want.[12] But such inferences violate the subordination principle. The evidence that all four objects are "murkle" contains evidence that one is green, one yellow, and one purple. This is evidence that "snarfs" are all either green, yellow, or purple; it is not discredited by further evidence; and its conclusion is incompatible with " 'Snarfs' are 'murkle.' " Consequently, the given evidence is bad evidence that the mask is red and we can avoid drawing an arbitrary conclusion.

The basic consideration that preserves the nonarbitrariness of projection is that sometimes reliable plausibility-conferring evidence is still bad evidence and hence cannot be good evidence against a competing conclusion. Moreover, it can be bad evidence even if it is not discredited by additional evidence, simply because it depends upon evidence that is not otherwise discredited and that supports a competing conclusion. This is why our evidence justifies projecting "green" rather than "grue" for emeralds. We have no good evidence against projecting "green" because our evidence for projecting "grue" turns out to be bad subordinate evidence. Thus, since our evidence for "green" is otherwise sound and reliable, we can be justifiably sure that all emeralds are green.

5. SUMMARY

The possibility of justification does require the possibility of confirmation. But fortunately confirmation is not as incoherent as it sometimes seems to be. Some principles that work for one form of confirmation fail to work for another, and when the forms are confused, the principles seem to be both indispensable and yet absurd.

Confirmation principles can also make it seem that generalizations and predictions are arbitrary, that competing projections are equally supported by our evidence. But a principle of bad evidence can be used to break the apparent deadlocks in intuitively satisfying ways. Hence the need for confirmation is not really an obstacle to knowledge.

CHAPTER ELEVEN

Foundations

1. THE SCEPTICAL ARGUMENT

We have considered two attacks on our justification for being sure of things. The first tries to link being sure with being dogmatic. The second maintains that we can never justifiably draw nondeductive conclusions. Let us now consider a third attack. It insists that justification requires having foundations that either are not available at all or are not plentiful enough to support many of our conclusions. Since the attack is often directed against the justification of beliefs, I shall examine it as such, bearing in mind that, if it succeeds, it also undermines our justification for being sure.

The sceptic typically presses his attack by insisting that few, if any, beliefs are immediately justifiable, that there are not enough foundational beliefs in this sense. Just what this claim might mean remains to be seen. But before analysing and assessing it, we should first consider whether the sceptic is right to assume that justification requires foundations. There are at least three ways of challenging his assumption: first, by letting something other than justified beliefs play the role that according to foundationalism immediately justifiable beliefs must play, viz., the role of terminating justificatory series; second, by denying that the terminating role has to be played at all, i.e., by allowing a series to go on indefinitely; and third, by denying that there are justificatory series, i.e., by appealing to some form of coherence. Let us consider each challenge in turn.[1]

2. NONFOUNDATIONAL TERMINI

One way to terminate a justificatory series without relying on foundations is to appeal to nonjustified terminating beliefs. For example, according to this view we justifiably believe that there was a First World War because we justifiably believe that we were told of it, and the latter belief is justified because we believe that we remember being told of it, where there is no justification for this last belief. But removing the justification of the starting point seems to destroy the justification of every other member of the series. Hence this proposal is not very attractive.

A less unattractive approach is to terminate the series in a nonbelief—e.g., in our memory of being told of the war, as distinct from our believing that we remember.[2] But it seems that not just any memory will get the job done. Even though we do remember, if we have a reliable reason to think that we don't remember, we are not justified in believing anything because of this particular memory. The belief that we remember must be at least potentially justified, in which case the sceptic will simply shift his attack. Instead of relying on foundational beliefs, we now have to rely on potential foundational beliefs. And the sceptic will probably insist that these are no more available than foundational beliefs. Thus, the problem is simply relocated, not solved.

3. AN INFINITE SERIES

Allowing potentially justified beliefs as members of a justificatory series might prompt someone to claim that a series can be endless. He might concede that no finite mind can hold an infinity of beliefs and then claim that we can still be in a position where, for each belief in an infinite set, we would have been justified in holding it had we held it and found it plausible. For example, if we justifiably believe that Fido is a dog, we are potentially justified in believing that Fido is not a cat, not a beetle, not a number, *ad infinitum*. If so, a series need have no terminus.[3]

This view is not as frivolous as it might first seem. Suppose that a sceptic replies that the view absurdly implies that every belief is justified, on the ground that an endless series can be constructed for any belief, including a belief's negation. But the possibility of constructing such a series simply means that a given belief is justified *if* each of its predecessors is justified. It does not mean that the belief *is* justified. Moreover, we can prefer one series over another, since the task is simply to justify beliefs, not series. Thus, we can proceed to defend a given belief, and reject its negation, by appealing to as many of its predecessors as it takes in practice. This process can in fact come to an end without the need for a theoretical terminus.

A sceptic might then argue that if we are to know that which we justifiably believe, we must also be justified in believing that our belief is justified, and that the infinity of a justificatory series would put this requirement beyond our reach. But satisfying the higher-order demand does not require our being justified in believing of each member of the series that it is justified. We need only be justified in holding the general metabelief that each member is justified, something we can accomplish inductively. At worst, this may imply that we must be potentially justified in holding an infinitely complex belief of the form "*p1* is justified because *p2* is justified because . . . ." But this simply means that *if* we held the belief and found it plausible, we would be justified in holding it. It does not mean that we *can* hold the belief. Thus, higher-order demands do not create insoluble problems.

There are three good reasons, however, for distrusting an appeal to an infinite series. First, although there is nothing wrong with the potential justification of an infinity of *consequent* beliefs, such as the beliefs entailed by "Fido is a dog," this does not establish the possible potential justification of an infinity of *prior* beliefs, i.e., an infinity of plausibility-conferring beliefs. In the case of consequent beliefs, we can appeal to the principle that evidence that justifies a belief also justifies anything clearly entailed by the belief. But there is no such principle in the case of prior beliefs. And a justificatory series is composed of prior beliefs.

Second, it is doubtful that, for every member of some infinite set of prior beliefs, I would have been justified in holding it if I had held it and found it plausible. It may be possible for me to satisfy this condition in theory. But in actual fact I doubt that I do. Thus, appealing to an infinite series itself borders on scepticism.

Third, when I consider actual beliefs that I take to be justified and then try to identify prior beliefs, the resulting chains tend to settle pretty quickly on beliefs about memories, observations, and the like. If justificatory series were infinite, one would expect a different result in practice.

4. COHERENCE

To be distinctive, a coherence theory must hold that, at the level at which foundationalism introduces immediately justifiable beliefs, no belief is prior to any other belief. Justification at that level must not be a matter either of a belief's being immediately justifiable or of its being justifiable because a prior belief is justifiable. The belief must be justifiable solely because it enters into a suitable coherence relationship. Moreover, to be effective, the theory must avoid implying that every belief enters into such a relationship. Finally, the theory must avoid making coherence so complicated that we cannot tell whether a given belief displays it. These are not easy demands for a theory to meet.

Lehrer adopts a coherence theory according to which justification is a matter of whether a belief is (or, given a responsible subject, would have been) believed to have the best chance of being true.[4] The belief is not justified as a result of the metabelief's being a prior justified belief. It is not that sort of relationship. Moreover, a belief and its negation cannot both be justifiably held by the same person, since no one can responsibly believe of both a belief and its negation that each has the best chance of being true. And we can then tell fairly easily whether a given belief is justified.

Nevertheless, as we have already seen (in chapter 9, section 3), the theory implies that a belief and its negation can both be justified if they are held by different persons, even if the persons share the same evidence. Furthermore, nothing is said about the epistemic status of the metabelief. If it is not justified, the justification of our other beliefs is in jeopardy. The metabelief cannot be immediately justifiable. And we cannot appeal to a metametabelief without generating a new infinite series. Consequently, many of the same problems seem to persist.

Rescher offers a coherence theory that "sees a cognitive system as a family of interrelated theses not necessarily of hierarchical arrangement, but rather linked among one another by an *interlacing network* of connections."[5] Yet he continues to view the connections as inferential and to talk of the provision of good evidential reasons. These notions usually have priority written right into them. For example, if our only good reason for expecting rain is that a reliable weatherman predicted it, we cannot cite the probability of rain as a good reason for saying that the weatherman predicted it. We need independent evidence of rain before we can do that. Thus, good reasons are asymmetrical in a way that works against a coherence theory. Moreover, Rescher feels the need to allow for a pragmatic justification of a whole network of beliefs, and this would probably move a sceptic to refocus his attack on the conditions of pragmatic justification. Finally, Rescher concedes a need to introduce data as surrogates for axiomatic foundations, and their positive nature is left unclear. Indeed, when he says that "a proposition will not qualify as a datum without *some* appropriate grounding," he might even be implying that something else can be prior to a datum, in which case he has not totally escaped the foundational model.[6] A sceptic will not be appeased unless the break with foundationalism is sharper than this.

Bonjour outlines a coherence theory that tries to allow for the adjudication of competing systems of beliefs by appealing to input. He claims that "there is no reason to think that one objective world will go on providing coherent input to incompatible systems in the long run."[7] But if such input really does lack epistemic priority, positive input for one system need never be negative input for an incompatible system. For example, a system that includes the belief in a Cartesian demon can permanently discredit observational input. Hence the system can assimilate objective input just as coherently as a rival system. There seems to be no way to avoid such a result without conferring priority on input and thereby reintroducing foundational considerations.

5. IMMEDIATE JUSTIFICATION

Thus, the only satisfactory response to a sceptic is to accept his challenge and show that we do have the foundations that we need for knowledge. But perhaps some will see another way. If the sceptic insists that no conclusion is ever justified, his remark applies to his own sceptical conclusion. Thus, his position is correct only if it is not justified. Some think that such self-refutation is fatal. But I doubt that it is. The sceptic can acknowledge the result and in a Pyrrhonian spirit continue to assert his conclusion, without pretending to be justified in asserting it. Such an attitude will be hard to understand by anyone who is disposed to assert something only if he finds the assertion justified. But this does not make the attitude either impossible or incoherent. Moreover, an ingenious sceptic might be able to allow enough foundational beliefs to support his own negative conclusions, while denying that there are enough to support the full range of conclusions we normally draw. Consequently, we do have to assess the sceptic's assertion that not enough foundational beliefs are available.

To do this, we first need definitions for some key expressions. Following the account in chapter 9, section 2 of what it is to be justifiably sure of something, let us say that we justifiably believe something if, and only if

(i) We find the belief plausible.
(ii) It is accordingly plausible.
(iii) We have no preponderant counterevidence.
(iv) Our evidence is reliable.

The difference between holding a justified belief and being justifiably sure is that we can have *some* good counterevidence in the case of justified belief, provided it is not preponderant. Similarly, reliability is then a matter of our evidence's being of a sort that is usually not augmented by preponderant counterevidence. The addition of slight counterevidence defeats a knowledge claim, but not a justified-belief claim.

We can say that our belief is *immediately justified* if, and only if

(i) We find the belief intuitively plausible.
(ii) It is intuitively plausible.
(iii) We have no preponderant counterevidence.
(iv) Our intuition is reliable.

Strictly, condition (iii) is now redundant on condition (ii), since a belief is intuitively plausible only if there is no good evidence against it. This means that an immediately justified belief is one of which we can be justifiably sure. It does not mean, however, that condition (iv) is redundant on condition (ii). We can intuit something in an unreliable way and, even though our intuition is correct, still fail to be justified in believing what we intuit; the chance of having to retract is then just too great.

We can say that a belief is *immediately justifiable,* or has a *potential immediate justification,* if and only if

> We would have been immediately justified in holding it if, *ceteris paribus,* we had in fact held it and found it intuitively plausible.

This means that a belief is immediately justifiable only if it is intuitively plausible and only if, had we found it intuitively plausible, our intuition would have been reliable. The latter condition in turn means that our intuitions of the relevant sort have generally survived the addition of new evidence. Thus, if I am poor at intuiting my own feelings, in the sense that my intuitions are often subsequently abandoned, a belief about one of my current feelings cannot be immediately justifiable in light of my evidence.

Finally, we can say that our belief is *mediately justified* if and only if

(i)   We find the belief plausible because of something else; in this sense, we have a ground for finding it plausible.
(ii) The belief is plausible, given this ground's plausibility.
(iii) We have no preponderant counterevidence.
(iv) Our evidence is reliable.

Condition (i) refers broadly to our finding something plausible because of something else, not just to our finding it derivatively plausible. Condition (i) thereby includes our finding something plausible because of what we observe or remember even though we do not actually derive its plausibility from that of our observing or remembering. In this sense, observing or remembering something can ground a plausibility judgment, just as an implicit premise can help ground a conclusion when we derive something's plausibility by taking the premise for granted. We need not be aware of either the observation or the assumption.

Since (i) is compatible with our also finding the given belief intuitively plausible, a belief can be both immediately and mediately justified; e.g., "6 × 6 = 36" can be immediately justified and also be justified on good authority. There is no intention of making the two categories exclusive.

6. FOUNDATIONALISM

Let "foundationalism" mean a theory that adopts these three central propositions:

(i)   Beliefs are justified either immediately or mediately.
(ii) For any mediately justified belief, believing the ground of its plausibility is at least potentially justified, thereby creating a justificatory series.
(iii) A justificatory series must at some point terminate in a belief that is at least immediately justifiable.

Foundationalism therefore holds that a justified belief that is not itself immediately justified must be grounded in such a way that a belief in the ground, or in a ground of the ground, or in a ground of that ground (but *not* indefinitely) is at least immediately justifiable. The theory does not insist, however, that we must at some point be immediately justifi*ed* in holding a terminating belief. For example, the belief that I observe a committee chairman enter the room can terminate a series that grounds my belief that the meeting will start soon, even though I do not believe that I observe what I do. It suffices if the belief is potentially immediately justified in light of my evidence.

Foundationalism does not regard terminating beliefs as incorrigible, in any sense that implies that their justification cannot be defeated, or as self-evident, in any sense that implies that their justification is independent of the reliability of our intuitions. Such beliefs are certain, since they are intuitively plausible. But certainty does not guarantee justification, since it does not guarantee either that the belief is intuitively plausible or that the intuition is reliable.

Indeed, terminating beliefs are not even self-justified, as this expression is sometimes understood. A self-justified belief can be justified to some degree quite apart from any indication of what the remaining evidence is like. But a belief is immediately justified only if there are no additional considerations that make our intuition untrustworthy. Consequently, we should avoid calling foundationalism in the present sense "modest foundationalism," since the latter expression is often tied to the notion of self-justification.[8]

Foundationalism does insist on more than observations or memories as the termini of justificatory series, since it insists that beliefs about such observations or memories must be immediately justifiable. At bottom, this may simply represent a decision as to how to use the word "justified," in view of its proposed link with an ideal sense of "knowledge." Someone who believes something because of what he observes does not justifiably believe it unless he is at least potentially justified in believing that he observes what he does. If we fail to impose this requirement, we fail to claim that our observation-grounded beliefs are justified in a way that will interest the sceptic. In short, we peg our justificatory standards too low.

This means that observation-grounded beliefs like "The clock has stopped ticking" are not themselves immediately justified, precisely because we have observational grounds for finding them plausible.[9] But unless we define "immediately justified" to yield such a result, we fail to create a concept that enables us to say what the sceptic denies, viz. that there are enough beliefs that are justified without being grounded in any way, not even in observations or memories. And if justification is to satisfy ideal standards, we must be prepared to say such a thing.

Another advantage of defining "immediately justified" to exclude observation-grounded beliefs is that it reduces the need for arbitrary applications. For example, Goodman introduces three beliefs—"That is a moving red patch," "That is a red cardinal," and "That is the fourth bird to arrive this morning"—and complains of the arbitrariness of selecting one or two as foundational.[10] If immediately justified beliefs included observation-grounded beliefs, he would be right. In the present sense, however, if we find all three beliefs plausible because of what we observe, none of them is immediately justifiable. On the other hand, if the first one is not about an external object but is simply about what we perceive immediately, we do not find the belief plausible because of what we observe and it, and it alone, counts as immediately justified. Or, if the second belief is not about an external object but simply reports the content of our observation, it too can be immediately justified. These are not arbitrary decisions.

Foundationalism faces two major questions. First, does it generate any regresses that are just as unwelcome as the one it tries to stop? Second, can it find enough foundational beliefs to support the knowledge claims we normally want to make?

7. AVOIDING NEW REGRESSES

Since immediate justification requires the reliability of an intuition, it requires the justification of further beliefs. For example, as Oakley points out, I am immediately justified in reporting "It appears to me that something is blue" only if I am also justified in believing that the phenomenal report is not simply the result of wishful thinking—indeed, more generally, only if I am justified in believing that "there are no factors present of a type which would probably cause error in judgments about immediate experience."[11] This may not be exactly right as it stands. But the further justification is at least necessary if the report's immediate justifiability is to support a knowledge claim, since we have knowledge only if we are justified in claiming that the requirements of knowing are satisfied. But if the further belief must be justified, and if its justification in turn involves a further justification, a new series *is* started, and one that has no obvious end in sight. Have we therefore created a new reason for being sceptical?

Before addressing this question, we should be clear that the immediate justification of a belief does terminate the kind of series it is designed to terminate, viz. a series of prior beliefs. For example, the belief "My wife walked our dogs" derives plausibility from that of "She just told me so," which derives its plausibility from "I just heard her tell me," which derives its from "I remember her just telling me," where the last belief is intuitively plausible. Immediate justification does manage to terminate this sort of series.

Now, the series generated by the dependence of "It appears to me that something is blue" on "This phenomenal report is not the product of wishful thinking" *is* endless. The latter belief is immediately justifiable, but only if the metareport "The report that the phenomenal report is not produced by wishful thinking is not produced by wishful thinking" is also immediately justifiable. And this series is endless. But we can in fact satisfy the condition that, for each report in such a series, we would have been immediately justified had we believed the report and found it intuitively plausible. And our intuitions of the relevant sort are generally reliable. Consequently, such a series does not need terminating, and a similar comment applies to other consequent series of this type. Although even immediate justification requires the justifiability of further beliefs, and although there is no finite number of such beliefs, we *can* satisfy this requirement in actual practice. Thus, the infinity of this series is not a cause for scepticism.

Foundationalism does not generate any other infinite series. Granted, immediate justification of a belief requires the justifiability of the metabelief that the belief is justified. And the metabelief is not itself immediately justifiable, since it involves the justifiability of believing that the intuition is reliable, and this cannot be immediate. But the belief in reliability can derive its plausibility from a memory report, and the latter is immediately justifiable. Hence this chain comes to a halt pretty quickly.

The immediate justification of a belief may also require the justifiability of the metabelief that the belief is *immediately* justified. Bonjour sees a difficulty in this requirement. He feels that the distinctive feature $\emptyset$ in virtue of which a belief is immediately justifiable "must constitute a reason for thinking that it is likely to some appropriate degree to be true." If he is right, we justifiably believe that belief B is immediately justified only if we can justifiably deploy the argument

B is $\emptyset$.
$\emptyset$ beliefs are likely to be true.
Therefore, B is likely to be true.

Bonjour thinks that the argument's two premises cannot both be *a priori* and that at least one of them requires a prior empirical premise, in which case a new infinite regress of prior beliefs is created.[12]

But if $\varnothing$ is intuitive plausibility, the first premise is itself intuitively plausible and hence requires no empirical ground. And the second premise *is a priori,* since, necessarily, an intuitively plausible belief is one for which any counterevidence is bad and hence is absolutely certain.

Alternatively, suppose that $\varnothing$ consists in the reliability of our intuiting B. The first premise then *is* empirical and a new series is generated. But as we have seen, the consequent beliefs in this series can be justifiable in the light of our evidence, even though they are endless. Consequently, Bonjour's objection raises no new difficulties and immediately justifiable beliefs do provide adequate termini.

8. SUBJECTIVE FOUNDATIONS

Are there enough immediately justifiable beliefs to underwrite all the knowledge claims we usually want to make? There are no restrictions in principle on the content of such beliefs, since there are no theoretical restrictions on what we can find intuitively plausible. For example, there are no theoretical obstacles to my intuiting your feelings, or to a seer's finding future events intuitively plausible. The question of immediate justification then depends upon whether these intuitions are correct and reliable, and such conditions can be satisfied in principle.

Nevertheless, although the theoretical boundaries are open, immediately justifiable contingent beliefs are in fact largely restricted to beliefs that are exclusively about one's own current plausibility-conferring states. The latter beliefs can be called *subjective reports,* in the technical sense that they entail nothing about the past or future and nothing about external objects or other minds. For example, "I observe a brown dog" is a subjective report only if it avoids implying that an external brown dog exists and that anything has existed or will exist. The question of whether there are enough foundational beliefs thus in effect becomes the question of whether there are enough foundational subjective reports.

Subjective reports provide adequate foundations only if they are a sufficient source of plausibility, both for what we claim to know and for the required epistemic claims. But this is not a serious problem. For example, the plausibility of "I observe that p" establishes p's plausibility, as does the plausibility of "I remember that p." And the plausibility of "I have no good counterevidence" and "I remember that this sort of evidence is reliable" can help establish the probable reliability of given evidence and hence the probable absence of good counterevidence. Reports will seem inadequate only if we mistakenly think that they must individually yield more—e.g., only if we think that "I observe that p" must by itself establish that p is to some degree justified.

Reports are foundational only if they can be immediately justified. But this is no problem. Again, there will seem to be a problem only if we think that foundational beliefs must have a more powerful status, that they must be incorrigible, or axiomatic, or at least self-justified.

Reports can be foundational even if they are merely *justifiable*. They do not have to be believed, nor do we have to find them plausible. The only requirement is that we would have been justified had we believed them and found them intuitively plausible. Even someone who lacks the concept of an observation can have an observation report as a foundation in this sense. Countless reports can satisfy such a requirement, whereas relatively few would satisfy the stiffer requirement of having to be actually justified.

Justifiably believing a report about oneself does not involve relying on introspective evidence.[13] I do not find the report "I observe that p" plausible because I introspect myself observing that p. This would ground the plausibility judgment in an introspective act and destroy the report's immediate justification. It would also create an infinite regress, since the same thing would then be said of the report "I introspect myself observing that p." But we are not forced to adopt a doctrine of introspective evidence. I do not find the report "I observe a pen on the table" plausible because of anything else. I simply find it plausible on its own. Hence my believing it *can* be justified immediately.

Reports will seem to provide a meager foundation if they are restricted to sensory reports. But they are much richer than this. They include observation reports, even very sophisticated ones like "I observe the eclipse starting." They also include reports of evidence like "I have no good counterevidence." And they include memory reports like "I remember that the square of the hypotenuse equals the sum of the squares of the other two sides." Their collective content is therefore diverse enough to support our knowledge claims.

Some will be unhappy about including memory reports as foundations. For example, Malcolm thinks that someone who remembers that p bears the same relationship to p as he originally did when he first learned that p, hence that someone who now remembers that he felt chest pains yesterday has no ground for believing that he felt them, given that yesterday he had no ground for the belief. Malcolm argues that remembering that p just is continuing to know that p, in which case it cannot be a ground for such knowledge.[14]

It is true that "I remember that p" can mean "I still know that p," and then Malcolm's comments are correct. But a memory sentence can also be used in other ways. For example, we can say "I remember it as being red, but my memory is unclear; hence I'm not sure; hence I don't know." Or we can remember things that are false because, although we remember what we are taught, the lesson was wrong. Or someone can be hypnotized to remember something that did not really happen. Or we can simply misremember things. A first-person memory sentence can be used to report memories of this sort, in which case it is not a disguised knowledge claim. It can then play a foundational role.

Thus, given that foundational reports need only be a source of plausibility, that they need not be axiomatic, that they need not be actually justified, that their justification does not involve introspection, and that they include more than sensory reports, there can be enough of them to support the knowledge claims we normally want to make.

9. SUMMARY

Sceptics argue that knowledge requires foundations and that this requirement cannot be justified. They are right about the requirement, but wrong to be pessimistic about its satisfaction. The necessary foundations consist in immediately justifiable beliefs. They do not generate new regresses, and there are enough of them to get the job done.

If foundationalism is right, empirical knowledge claims are justified only if our observations are not discredited by general features of perception. Let us now see whether a sceptic can find anything harmful in the nature of perception.

CHAPTER TWELVE

Perception

1. INTRODUCTION

A foundational view of empirical knowledge can seem to create the following problem. Our observations are partly a function of our immediate perceptions—that is, we observe what we do partly because of what we immediately perceive. As a result, anything that tends to drive an epistemic wedge between our immediate perceptions and external objects thereby tends to discredit our observations as evidence of an external world. There is a theory of perception that does just that. The aim of this chapter is to articulate and assess that theory.

2. PERCEPTION AND OBSERVATION

Let us decide to use our perceptual terminology in a way that yields four potentially useful results: First, "see," "hear," "feel," "smell," and "taste" refer to species of perceiving, not to species of observing. Second, whereas we can both observe a thing and observe that something is the case, we can only perceive a thing, not perceive that something is the case; e.g., we cannot hear that the enemy has declared war. Third, we cannot observe anything without making use of concepts, whereas perception does not require concepts; e.g., an infant can feel warmth without having the concept "warmth." Fourth, observation requires some degree of attention, perception does not; e.g., a brain-damage victim can see triangles without even being disposed to believe that triangles exist.

I think that such decisions are coherent, although I shall not try to defend their coherence here.

3. IMMEDIATE PERCEPTION

Let us say that we *immediately perceive* something if, and only if, we perceive it in such a way that we can find our perceiving it intuitively plausible. For example, when we see a yellow after-image, we immediately see something yellow because we can find

"I see something yellow" intuitively plausible. Thus, a report of what we immediately perceive is capable of being immediately justifiable in light of our evidence.

The things we immediately perceive share with Berkeley's ideas the feature that we can perceive them without having any background experience, say, when we first acquire a sensory capacity.[1] For example, someone who suddenly gains his hearing can immediately hear sounds when a coach approaches, but he does not hear the coach unless he has suitable background information. Yet contrary to what Berkeley suggests, this does not mean that the coach cannot be heard in a proper or strict sense. There are occasions when what we say we perceive should be restricted to what we immediately perceive, e.g., when we should concede "I saw only a blur, not a propellor." But there are also occasions when we can quite properly say that we saw a propellor and not merely a blur. The boundaries of immediate perception are not the boundaries of the proper usage of perceptual words.

Although someone who immediately perceives something can intuit that he does, he need not do so. Indeed, there is a sense in which he might be unable to do so, e.g., if he lacks the necessary concepts or intelligence. Intuition is possible only in the sense that the perception involved is of a sort to be intuited by the perceiver. This means that the perceiver need not know that he perceives what he does. The things we immediately perceive are unlike Price's sense data, which are such that the perceiver cannot doubt their existence.[2] And they are unlike Malcolm's objects of direct perception, which are objects of which we can have incorrigible knowledge.[3] This does not mean, however, that they lose all their epistemological significance. They are still such that the perceiver can have an intuitive knowledge of their existence, which means that they can play a foundational role to this extent.

Some feel that an account of immediate perception should not prejudge an answer to the question "What sorts of things do we immediately perceive?" The feeling is well founded if by a neutral account we mean one that leaves conceptual room for the question to arise. But it goes too far if it means that the account cannot allow us to make a pretty quick assessment of an answer. For example, Jackson thinks that an account should not prejudge whether in seeing a white cat in pink light we immediately see something white or something pink.[4] The present account satisfies this demand to the extent that it leaves conceptual room in which to argue that what we immediately see is white. We do have room to argue that we can find "I see something white" intuitively plausible in such circumstances. But the argument is not at all convincing, since it seems pretty obvious that we find "There is something white, which I see" plausible because of what we otherwise know about the lighting and about how white objects generally look in pink light. Hence the account leads to a quick resolution of this question.

4. EXTERNAL OBJECTS

Let us use "external object" in the most demanding way possible, to mean an object the existence of which is entirely independent of being perceived. If a description of a perceiver's state and circumstances does not itself entail that a given external object is perceived, the object can exist unperceived regardless of how good the conditions for perceiving objects are. For example, an external pen can exist unseen even if someone sighted is standing right in front of it, has his eyes open, is looking in its direction, there is no obstruction, the light is bright, and so on. Granted, in such circumstances the person might be justifiably sure that no external pen exists. But this condition does not entail that no external pen exists. Conversely, it is logically possible for someone to be justifiably sure that he sees an external pen in front of him when in fact there is no such object. Indeed, it is logically possible for him to be permanently justified and for no such object to exist.

This makes the concept of an external object potentially more demanding than the concept of a public object, i.e., of an object that is capable of being perceived by more than one person. For example, there is room to argue that a mirror image is a public object but not an external object. Similarly, the concept of externality is potentially more demanding than the concept of mind independence. For instance, someone might be prepared to say that, although a given mind-independent object can exist unperceived in many circumstances, there are some circumstances in which its not being perceived is a *logically* conclusive reason for denying its existence. In that case the mind-independent object is not an external object.

Now, whether objects like pens and rocks are external can be a matter for philosophical inquiry. But in this context we are interested in whether we can be justifibly sure that there are external objects, not merely with whether we can be justifiably sure that there are public, mind-independent objects. Accordingly, we are interested in whether we can be justifiably sure of the existence of pens and rocks even if they are conceived as external objects. As a result, let us simply decide to use words like "pen" and "rock" to refer to external objects whenever they are used to refer to objects at all.

5. WHAT WE IMMEDIATELY PERCEIVE

We can never immediately perceive external objects, since we cannot find "I perceive x" intuitively plausible when x is an external object. For example, I find it plausible that I see an external ashtray on the table in front of me partly because I find it plausible that I have visual evidence of the ashtray's existence. Perceiving an external object involves having good perceptual evidence of the object's existence, in which case a claim to perceive the object must be grounded in a claim to have such evidence.

Some will distrust such a hierarchical view of evidence. For example, Austin argues that evidence for external-object statements is usually formulated in terms of external objects and that, "in general, *any* kind of statement could state evidence for *any* other kind, if the circumstances were appropriate."[5] He is right about how the evidence for an external-object statement is *usually* formulated, and he is right that external-object statements *can* be used to provide evidence for other kinds of statements, including subjective reports. But he is wrong if he thinks that sometimes perceiving an external object does not involve having perceptual evidence of its existence. For instance, he says that someone who sees a pig in plain view does not thereby have evidence of the pig's existence, unlike someone who relies on prints, sounds, or smells. Now, it is true that someone who initially smells a pig and then sees it come into plain view will probably not say "I now also have visual evidence of the pig's existence," since this is a potentially misleading understatement. Normally he will say "I now see the pig," which implies that he is justified in believing that the pig exists. But suppose that he knows that there are pig facsimiles in the area. He can then make the visual-evidence claim without being misleading, and in both instances the claim is true. Seeing the pig does involve having visual evidence. And someone finds it plausible that he sees the pig partly because he finds it intuitively plausible that he has such evidence. As a result, he does not immediately see the pig.

6. REPRESENTATIONALISM

Some think that having perceptual evidence of external objects consists in immediately perceiving internal objects, in the sense of objects that cannot exist unperceived and cannot be perceived by more than one person.[6] Three reasons can lead to such a conclusion.

First, it can seem that, whenever we perceive an external object, we perceive something, x, such that (a) we can intuit that we perceive x, (b) our perceiving x provides evidence of the external object's existence, and (c) x is not an external object and hence is an internal object. For example, it can seem that when I see external objects on my desk, I see various colours and shapes such that I can intuit that I see such colours and shapes, my seeing them helps to provide evidence of the existence of my desk and the objects on it, and the colours and shapes are internal objects.

Second, it can seem that, whenever we perceive an external object, the object sensibly looks or appears some way, $\varnothing$, to us—as distinct frcm its conceptually looking *to be* $\varnothing$ to us—and that this consists in our immediately perceiving a $\varnothing$ internal object. For example, it can seem that whenever we see an external ripe tomato, the tomato looks red to us, in which case we also immediately see an internal red object.

Third, it can seem that situations involving illusions or hallucinations do involve the immediate perception of internal objects and that every perceptual situation must therefore involve the immediate perception of such objects. For instance, if I immediately see two internal penlike objects when I press my eyeball while looking at an external pen, I also immediately see several other objects spatially related to the internal penlike objects and together they form an immediate visual field. Some of the field's occupants continue to exist even after I stop having double vision and they form a visual field with other immediate objects. It can seem, then, that even in veridical cases we immediately see internal objects. Moreover, analogous considerations also seem to apply to nonvisual cases.

Philosophers impressed by such considerations will sometimes go on to conclude that perceiving an external object is like seeing an object by seeing a picture of the object. According to this view, we never immediately perceive the external object itself;

we perceive only an internal representative. Call such a view a *representational theory* of perception.[7]

If representationalism is right, a serious problem arises concerning the status of the evidence provided by our immediate perceptions. When we see a literal picture of an object, we can acquire background information that lets us decide whether the picture is a good likeness. Acquiring such information eventually involves someone's being able to compare the picture with the original, or at least to compare some picture with some original. But there is nothing analogous to this in the case of immediately perceiving inner representatives, since *ex hypothesi* we can never immediately perceive the represented objects. Consequently, if representationalism is right, the question arises as to how we can say that our immediate perceptions afford good evidence concerning the external world. If we cannot say that they do, we cannot say that our observations concerning external objects are worth anything, since their worth depends upon the worth of the perceptions on which they are based. Indeed, we cannot even claim to perceive external objects, since such perceptual claims imply that we have good sensory evidence of external objects. Representationalism thus places our empirical knowledge claims in serious jeopardy.

7. PHENOMENA AND OBJECTS

There are various possible reactions to the problem. We could revert to direct realism and insist that we do immediately perceive external objects. But this has little independent support. We could try phenomenalism, insisting on a closer conceptual link between objects and the things we immediately perceive. But this is to abandon the externality of objects. Or we could retain representationalism and argue that an external-world hypothesis best explains what we immediately perceive. But this sacrifices the certainty of an external world. Finally, we could adopt a nonrelational analysis of immediate perception, arguing that it does not involve our being related to things of any sort, internal or otherwise. But as Jackson shows, this analysis has difficulties with cases in which someone simultaneously perceives something $\emptyset$ and perceives something non-$\emptyset$, and it cannot preserve the distinction between perceiving something $\emptyset$ and μ and both perceiving something $\emptyset$ and perceiving something μ.

A more promising solution is to look more carefully at the nature of the things we immediately perceive. Thus far we have left unchallenged the crucial assumption that, if a relational account is right, such things must be internal objects. Is such an assumption sound?

Imagine that I now see a yellow after-image. A reference to the yellow thing I thereby see is *essential* in the special sense that the thing to which we refer just *is* the yellow thing I now see. We cannot coherently suppose that *it* might have been seen by someone else instead of me or by me at a different time. Such a supposition violates a necessary condition of referring to that particular thing. The supposition is just as referentialy incoherent as "This individual might have been a numerically different individual in different circumstances." Let us call the yellow thing I thereby see a *phenomenon*. A $\emptyset$ phenomenon is therefore something that is perceived such that its identity consists in its being the $\emptyset$ thing perceived by a given person at a given time.

A phenomenon cannot exist unperceived. But we should be clear that this is a requirement of a phenomenon's very identity, not just a requirement of its being the kind of thing it is. For example, the necessary link between being a phenomenon and being perceived is different from that between being a triangle and having three sides. We can mistakenly say "This triangle has three sides, but *it* might have had four sides" and still be referring to the same triangle throughout. But we cannot sustain a coherent reference throughout "This yellow phenomenon is seen by me, but *it* might have been seen by someone else instead." This means that the phenomenal referring expression "the yellow thing I now see" is more than just a "rigid designator" in Kripke's sense. The designator "that $\emptyset$ thing" is rigid provided we cannot say "It might not have been $\emptyset$." But it is essential only if, more specifically, we cannot make such a remark *and* be referring to the same thing.[8]

Phenomena resemble some mental items in this respect. For instance, the reference "my previous thought of a triangle" is essential because the referent just *is* my thought of a triangle at a given time. Indeed, the reference "my seeing a yellow thing then" is also essential. But this does not mean that we should drop the distinction between a phenomenon and someone's perceiving a phenomenon. As we shall see in the next section, phenomena do not exist in the same time order as our perceptions.

Let us now use "object" in a technical sense, as a deliberate foil for "phenomenon." An *object* can be referred to nonessentially as the $\emptyset$ thing perceived by a given person at a given time. External things are therefore objects in this technical sense, as are public and mind-independent things. And even things that cannot exist unperceived can be objects, provided this is not a condition on their identity—that is, even if "This yellow thing is seen by me, but *it* might have been seen by you" is logically mistaken, it involves a reference to an object if the pronoun "it" sustains the reference. In that case the object is internal.

Immediately perceiving something consists in perceiving a phenomenon—that is, if we perceive x in such a way that we can find "I perceive x" intuitively plausible, our reference to x as "the $\emptyset$ that I now perceive" must be essential. Since the distinction between numerical and qualitative identity does apply to phenomena, they are entities. Hence our perceiving them does involve our being related to entities, and to that extent a relational analysis of immediate perception is correct. But phenomena are not objects, not even internal objects. Consequently, although a relational analysis holds, the things we immediately perceive are not internal objects in a technical sense of "objects."

Before determining whether this result removes the epistemological problems that confront representationalism, we should confirm the potentially controversial view that having perceptual evidence does consist in perceiving phenomena.

8. PERCEIVING EXTERNAL OBJECTS

I think that representationalism is right about this much, that having perceptual evidence *is* a matter of immediately perceiving things that are not external objects. Although such a view implies that perceiving external objects always involves immediately perceiving something, there are three reasons for welcoming such a result.

First, in any perceptual situation, we can always report perceiving something in such a way that we can find the report intuitively plausible. For example, when I see a ripe tomato, I can say "I see something red" in such a way that I can find the remark intuitively plausible. Granted, I could use the same sentence to refer to the tomato I see, in which case I would not be describing an immediate perception. But I can also use it to make an intuitively plausible report, and in that case I do describe an immediate perception.

Second, whenever we perceive an external object, the object looks or appears ∅ to us, in which case we immediately perceive something ∅. Correlating appearances with immediately perceived things does not reify appearances, since it does not imply that we perceive appearances. If a penny looks elliptical to us, we do not see the penny's elliptical look. We merely see something elliptical in such a way that we can find the visual report intuitively plausible. Of course, we must remember that how an object looks is distinct from how it looks *to be*. If a distant mountain looks to us to be very large, we do not thereby immediately see something very large; indeed, what we immediately see has no size in relation to the size of objects, only in relation to other things we immediately see.[9]

Third, the representationalist's generalization argument for saying that we always immediately perceive internal pictures of external objects does manage to establish that any perceptual situation involves immediate perception. If we immediately perceive things when we hallucinate or suffer double vision, we also immediately perceive things in more normal situations. Austin is suspicious about such an extrapolation. For example, he argues that there is not enough qualitative similarity between seeing a mirage and seeing a real oasis, and that qualitative similarity fails to establish generic sameness in any case.[10] But the generalization argument does not rely on qualitative similarity. It appeals to spatial connections between things that are admittedly immediately perceived and things that await metaphysical categorization. For instance, if we see a real camel while seeing a mirage, we see something camel-like beside something oasislike; since the latter is seen immediately, so is the former. This type of extension is unharmed by Austin's objections.

Some might feel, however, that, although perceiving external objects does involve immediately perceiving things, it does not involve perceiving phenomena, notwithstanding earlier objections to a nonrelational analysis of immediate perception. They might feel that, if the choice is strictly between a nonrelational analysis and the conclusion that perceiving external objects always involves perceiving phenomena, the former option is the lesser of two evils. Let me try to anticipate some of their objections.

Critics of sense data might argue that since phenomena are entities, they must be determinate, and then deny that the things we immediately perceive are determinate. Now, a phenomenon can be indeterminate in the sense that it is a borderline case; e.g., it is neither red nor nonred because of its location on the colour spectrum. But this type of indeterminancy can characterize any entity and is no problem. Beyond this, a phenomenon is determinate within its own category. For example, an after-image cannot be, or fail to be, a mile from Montreal, but this is because it is not an object. By the same token, a cat is neither valid nor invalid because it is not an argument. The after-image is no more indeterminate on this account than a cat. On the other hand, for any predicate that attaches to phenomena without absurdity, a given phenomenon either has it or fails to have it—unlike something we think of; e.g., although we can think of a large cat, the cat I think of need be neither large nor small. Thus, if someone sees a speckled hen, indeterminacy can characterize how he sees the hen *as,* but not the henlike phenomenon he immediately sees. If he sees the hen as a uniformly white rooster, because he has been told that it is a white rooster in disguise, he then does not see anything with an indefinite number of speckles. Yet what he immediately sees remains the same. Similarly, indeterminacy can characterize the way an object looks to us to be, or the way we take it to be; but this does not mean that the way it looks, or the phenomenon involved, is indeterminate.[11]

If phenomena are entities, they must be capable of persistence, and this requirement might seem to create problems. For example, if I blink my eyes while looking at a ripe tomato, it might seem an intolerably arbitrary matter as to whether a single red phenomenon survives the blink.[12] But if there is a short interval during which I do not immediately see anything, there is one clear sense in which no phenomenon can survive the blink, since there is a break in phenomenal time. Phenomenal continuity in this sense is strictly a matter of whether a given phenomenon continues to be perceived. Thus, I stop seeing one red phenomenon when my lids close, and start seeing another one when they open. Of course, other uses of "same phenomenon" are possible, some of which would allow continuity in this type of example. But such leeway is also possible in the case of *bona fide* entities; e.g., some uses of "same person" can allow a bodily takeover by an alien intelligence. Similarly, although phenomenal persistence clearly allows for qualitative change, there are cases where it is hard to decide between persistence and replacement; e.g., whether a red square suddenly shrinks and changes to a yellow dot or is suddenly replaced by a yellow dot. But there are equally puzzling cases concerning objects; e.g., whether a body can survive the instantaneous replacement of all its parts, or whether an organism can survive transformations from fertilized ovum to zygote to embryo to fetus. Persistence is not a greater source of consternation in the case of phenomena than it is in the case of objects.[13]

Some might think that we cannot preserve the division between phenomena and objects if we locate phenomena in space, in which case phenomena cannot be aligned with what we immediately perceive, and the whole hierarchical scheme collapses. But assigning spatial properties to phenomena does not put them in the space of objects, precisely because phenomena are not objects at all. Even the human body I immediately feel just *is* the body felt by me now and is not an object. It should not be confused with *my* body, which is an object in public space, not a phenomenon in my kinaesthetic-tactile field.

The temporal nature of phenomena might seem to create problems of a different sort. We do not immediately perceive anything instantaneous, except the beginnings and endings of things. We perceive things either enduring or in succession; e.g., we do not successively hear instantaneous sounds, but hear successive sounds, each of which lasts for some time. But if we now hear a series of sounds, the earliest sound in the series is one we have already heard, which seems to put it in our past. Yet because we now hear it immediately, it also seems to be in our present, which appears to contradict the previous result. Thus, the temporal structure of phenomena might seem to harbor a contradiction.[14]

The apparent contradiction can be removed by noting that, although some phenomena are temporally interrelated—e.g., one sound can follow another sound—they cannot be located in the same time order as that of objects or, therefore, of mental subjects. For instance, imagine that I look at a traffic light and see a green phenomenon follow a red one. The time of the phenomenal change cannot be related to the time of the light's changing. Otherwise we could refer to the green phenomenon as the green thing that begins to exist just after the light changes, which would give it an identity apart from its being the green thing seen by me at the given time. In that case we could say that the green thing I then see—i.e., the green thing that begins seconds after the light changes—might have been seen by someone else instead, in which case the green thing would not be a phenomenon. A definite description that relates an ostensible phenomenon to an event in public time is different from a description like "the brightest green phenomenon seen by anyone." We can say "The green phenomenon that I now see is the brightest one seen by anyone" and concede "I might not have seen the brightest one," without implying "I might not have seen the one I do see." We can avoid the latter implication by insisting that the only result is "The one I now see might not have been the brightest." But we cannot take such a way out if we say "The green phenomenon that I now see is the one starting a few seconds after the light change." The concession "I might not have seen the one starting then" does allow "The one I see might not have started then." Thus, phenomena cannot be coherently located in our present or in our past, and the apparent contradiction does not arise. Nothing in the temporal nature of phenomena prevents them from being the things we immediately perceive.

Finally, since phenomena are entities, they satisfy any existential requirements of immediate perception. For example, whereas Ayer suggests that a phenomenal report uses a perceptual term in a nonexistential sense, Austin correctly rejects such a suggestion, claiming, e.g., that "I see a speck" does imply the speck's existence.[15] But Austin is wrong to go on to suggest that if we make the report when we see a star and then say "The speck is a star," we correctly identify something we immediately see with an external star. Our remark is correct only if it means that the external object we see in virtue of immediately seeing the speck is a star. This reading preserves the numerical difference between the phenomenal speck and the external star.

Adopting this view has the added advantage of not having to concede, with Austin, that when we say "I see two pencil-like things" in a double-vision case, our use of "see" is being stretched to avoid implying existence. Our report does imply the existence of two phenomena, although it does not imply the existence of two objects.

Thus, there are no good reasons for thinking that the things we immediately perceive are not phenomena. Treating them as phenomena avoids implying that we immediately perceive internal objects. We can defend the determinacy and persistence of the things we immediately perceive. We can assign a coherent spatial and temporal character to such things. And we thereby usefully preserve their existence. The question now is "Do we also thereby avoid the epistemological problems that confront representationalism?"

9. PHENOMENAL EVIDENCE AND EMPIRICAL KNOWLEDGE

Regarding the things we immediately perceive as phenomena eliminates the source of a picture theory of perceptual evidence. If such things were internal objects and hence had an identity apart from being the things we perceive, they would stand to us epistemically in something like the way pictures stand to us. We would then have to find some independent way of authenticating their evidential status, which, as we have seen, is a difficult task.

By regarding them as phenomena, however, we eliminate the need for an independent authentication. Phenomena are not like pictures because they are not objects, not even internal ones. Hence the question of whether our perceiving phenomena affords good evidence of the existence of similar external objects is not a question of whether there is a good likeness between phenomena and external objects. It is simply a question of what the remaining evidence in each particular instance is like. For instance, it is a question of what we otherwise immediately perceive, of what we observe, and of what we remember. For example, the question of whether my seeing a square phenomenon is strong evidence of the existence of a square object is not a question of whether square phenomena have been independently correlated with square objects, or of whether supposing that there is a square object best explains what I see. It is a question of whether I fail to feel a square phenomenon, whether I remember that my eyesight is good, whether I observe myself touching a square object, whether I observe no one dissenting, and so on.

Locke's reference to the "testimony of the senses" introduces an apt analogy in this connection.[16] Assessing phenomenal evidence is like assessing testimonial evidence. We do have to look beyond the testimony to establish that it is good, strong, or reliable evidence. But we do not have to establish that it represents a higher authority. We can simply treat it as conferring plausibility on conclusions about objects, and then determine the further worth of those conclusions by looking at the remaining evidence. If in some situations our total evidence justifies saying that there is no good counterevidence, we are then justified in being sure of our conclusions. Nothing in the nature of perception itself prevents us from arriving at such a position.

Granted, our language is not well designed for describing phenomena independently of references to the objects they help to disclose. For instance, we often have to say that the phenomena are cuppish or cuplike. But this is because we are usually interested in talking about objects, not about phenomena. Indeed, it is precisely because phenomena help to provide good evidence of external objects that we rarely need to devise independent descriptions. And there is no reason to think that in principle such descriptions could not be found.

Granted too, perceiving phenomena is nonconceptual. But the having of evidence need not be a conceptual matter, since someone who has it need not know he has it or know what to do with it. The fact that a dog immediately sees something bonelike is evidence of the existence of a bone, even though the dog has few conceptual resources for making good use of such evidence. Similarly, a witness's observations can be discredited by poor eyesight, even though poor eyesight is simply a lack of fit between what the witness immediately sees and the way things really are. His observations are then based on poor visual evidence.

Regarding the perception of phenomena as evidence of an external world implies, e.g., that my seeing a red phenomenon is evidence of the existence of a red object, in the sense that the plausibility of the phenomenal report implies the plausibility of the object-statement. It does not imply that the report itself justifies the object-statement. Justification in this instance depends upon whether considerations that favour classifying colours as secondary qualities establish that we are never justified in assigning colours to objects. This question is not to be resolved simply by a consideration of the general nature of perception. Its resolution depends upon whether a scientific account of colour vision discloses an unreliability that destroys our justification for assigning colours. Yet such an account must leave some of our immediate perceptions sufficiently untainted that the observations that support the account are not themselves undermined. Otherwise the account would be self-refuting and hence ineffective. Thus, even if additional empirical considerations do call into question the worth of our phenomenal evidence, they cannot completely deprive us of empirical knowledge. Only a philosophical account of the nature of perception can do that; and as we have seen, such an account is mistaken.

10. THE POSSIBILITY OF MATERIAL OBJECTS

Defending the claim to have empirical knowledge of an external world involves one final task. If Berkeley is right, the very concept of an object that both resembles an idea and is external—i.e., the concept of a *material* object—is self-contradictory, in which case knowledge of the existence of such objects is impossible. He argues, in effect, that if an object resembles an idea—say, because they are both extended—there is no coherent reason to think that we can never immediately perceive the object, or a part of the object, since we do immediately perceive extended things; hence there is no coherent reason to think that the object is not itself an idea or at least composed of ideas. In that case no object could be like an idea without being an idea or being composed of ideas, which rules out material objects. In short, assigning common properties to objects and ideas breaks down the categorial division between the two.[17]

We avoid this result by treating the things we immediately perceive as phenomena and not as internal objects. We then have an answer to the question of why an extended object cannot be immediately perceived, given that we do immediately perceive extended things. The things we immediately perceive are not objects. They have no identity apart from being the things we immediately perceive on given occasions. Thus, although a given object is extended, and although we do immediately perceive extended things, we have a reason for thinking that the object cannot be something we immediately perceive. Hence the fact that external objects resemble phenomena does nothing to put them in the same category as phenomena, and the concept of a material object remains coherent.

11. SUMMARY

Our observations and memories are indispensable to our being justified in claiming knowledge of an external world. They can play an effective role in this respect, however, only if the perceptual evidence on which they depend is worthwhile. Representationalism casts doubt on the worth of such evidence by construing it as the immediate perception of internal pictures, a view that forces us to authenticate such pictures. Critics of representationalism hold either that we do immediately perceive external objects, or that we should dispense with references to external objects, or that immediate perception is nonrelational, or that perceiving external objects does not involve immediately perceiving anything. Each alternative confronts serious difficulties.

A better option analyses perceptual evidence as the immediate perception of phenomena. This is a relational analysis that nonetheless avoids the representationalist's epistemological model. Such a view allows us to accept the perception of phenomena as good evidence without first having to authenticate it. Moreover, any empirical evidence that discredits given phenomenal evidence must avoid undermining its own foundations. Hence nothing can discredit our phenomenal evidence so thoroughly that we are never justified in claiming empirical knowledge. In other words, whereas scientific arguments for disclaiming empirical knowledge might succeed in specified cases, philosophical arguments for universally disclaiming empirical knowledge are unsuccessful.

CHAPTER THIRTEEN

Access to Truth

1. THE POSSIBILITY OF TRUTH

Since knowledge involves truth, any threat to truth is a threat to knowledge. Now, Unger tries to establish the impossibility of truth by arguing both that truth involves an agreement with "the whole truth about the world" and that there cannot be any such thing as the whole truth about the world.[1] But his argument relies on the premise that the whole truth about the world is a metaphysical entity, a premise he fails to support effectively. Truth uncontentiously involves agreement with global truth only if the latter simply consists in everything that could be said such that what would thus be said actually is the case. But there is no reason to think that a reference to everything that could thus be said is a reference to an entity in a contentious sense.

What-clauses can similarly be used to paraphrase various sentences that according to Unger reveal the metaphysical nature of truth. Consider

> The truth about whether China is larger than India is that China is larger than India.
> The first thing he uttered was a truth, but the truth was not as informative as the lies he told later.
> The truth of what he said cannot be denied, and truth should always be valued.
> At first, I didn't think he was telling me the truth, but then I remembered the truth about it all and realized that he was.

These sentences can be paraphrased, respectively, as

> What could be asserted as to whether China is larger than India, such that what would be asserted actually is the case, is that China is larger than India.
> The first thing he uttered was of such a kind that what was thereby uttered actually is the case, but what he first uttered was not as informative as what he on a number of occasions

    later uttered, where what he later uttered was intended to be
    such that what was thereby uttered actually is not the case.
  It cannot be denied that what he said actually is the case, and
    whatever is said, such that what is said actually is the case,
    should always be valued.
  At first, I didn't think that what he was telling me actually is
    the case, but then I remembered what actually is the case
    about it all and realized that what he was telling me actually
    is the case.

These sentences do not refer to any entities except China, India, the utterer, and me. Similarly, we can remove the appearance of entity reference by paraphrasing "That is in agreement with the truth" as "That actually is the case," and "There's a lot of agreement with the truth in what you said" as "A lot of what you said actually is the case." Consequently, contrary to Unger, we need not regard references to the whole truth about the world as references to an entity. Indeed, I suspect that, were he to show otherwise, he would thereby remove the unattractiveness of accepting the existence of such an entity. Thus, we can continue to claim the truth of things, and the need for truth poses no threat to knowledge claims.

2. JUSTIFYING TRUTH CLAIMS

Since a knower must be justified in claiming knowledge, he must be justified in claiming that the conditions of knowledge are satisfied, including any truth conditions. Since truth is absolute, some will see a difficulty in this. Absolute certainty does not entail absolute truth, and finding something absolutely certain is therefore not to find it absolutely true. As a result, some might think that being justified in claiming absolute truth involves going beyond the evidence that justifies our being sure. And this seems a hopeless task.

Comparison theories of truth are particularly vulnerable to this problem. They hold that we determine truth not by establishing a proposition's coherence with other propositions or its utility in coping with subsequent experiences, but by comparing it with the objective reality that makes the proposition true. The analogy of comparing a picture with its original, or a map with its territory, is often used. Yet nothing analogous to the independent checking of an original or a territory seems possible. This is why someone like

Peirce is moved to replace the conception of an absolutely true opinion by one of an "opinion that is fated to be ultimately agreed to by all who investigate."[2]

Lehrer's solution is to point out that we merely have to satisfy the conditions of knowledge in order to have knowledge; we do not first have to establish that they are satisfied.[3] But if a condition of knowing is that we must be justified in claiming knowledge, we must be justified in claiming that the conditions of knowing are satisfied. Hence the problem remains.

We can solve the problem by enlisting the *principle of implicit justification.*

> If we are justified in believing p and also justified in believing "p entails q," we are justified in believing q.

The principle does not imply that we must justifiably believe everything clearly entailed by what we justifiably believe. But it does imply that, if we do not believe the entailed proposition, we would have been justified had we believed it.

Given this principle, our being justifiably sure of a proposition guarantees that we are justified in being sure of the proposition's truth, since we are justified in being sure that p entails "p is true." Although certainty does not entail truth, being justified in finding something certain does entail being justified in claiming its truth. Thus, there is no need to step outside the evidence that justifies our being sure in order to gain access to absolute truth. There is no need to compare a proposition with objective fact in order to tell that it is true.

Unfortunately, not everyone accepts the principle of implicit justification. Lehrer suggests that the principle is invalidated by a case in which we justifiably believe p, suddenly justifiably deduce q from p, and then, because we independently dislike q, become disenchanted with p. He thinks that there might be a time when we still justifiably believe both p and the entailment without justifiably believing q.[4] Now, if justification were simply a matter of belief, there would be such a contingency. But as we have seen, justification need not be conceived so subjectively (see chapter 9, section 3). Consequently, either we are no longer justified in believing p because we now have strong anti-q evidence that is also against p, or we are now justified in believing q because our ostensible anti-q evidence is outweighed or discredited by our pro-p evidence.

Wolgast introduces an interesting case in which we claim

knowledge that p, know that p entails q, and yet disclaim knowledge that q. For example, we say "I know that that's a watch and that a watch must contain works, but I don't know that it has works because I haven't looked inside it."[5] The same remark would hold for justified belief and this might seem to invalidate the principle. But as Wolgast points out, when we disclaim knowledge of the watch's insides, we are merely indicating that we have no independent evidence to support the entailed proposition. This simply means that we cannot claim knowledge of the watch's insides in any ordinary fashion without being misleading. It does not mean that we would not be justified in believing that there are works inside.

Richman criticizes the principle on the ground that standards for determining justification are sufficiently variable that a belief can be justified by given evidence when an entailed belief is not. For example, he thinks that if p is a prehistorical theory and q is "either p or $2 + 2 = 4$," evidence that justifies p can fail to justify q.[6] Now, he is right to think that standards do vary with given purposes. But in this context our purposes are philosophical and standards are uniformly demanding (see chapter 3, section 7). Consequently, if by present standards we justifiably believe p, we are by those same standards justified in believing the entailed disjunction, even if a better independent case for the disjunction can also be found via intuition.

Thalberg objects to the principle because he thinks that if p is the false "Jones will get the job and he has ten coins" and q the true "The man who'll get the job has ten coins," our evidence for p has no bearing on q's status. In that case p's being justified does not entail q's being justified.[7] Thalberg's position is based partly on the assumption that q is the general proposition that *whoever will be hired* has ten coins. But if q is entailed by p, q is not as general as this. For instance, the general proposition entails "If Smith is the man who will get the job, Smith has ten coins," and the latter proposition is not entailed by p. Granted, q *is* less definite than p, in the sense that there are propositions other than p such that if they are true, q is true—including the proposition "Smith will get the job and he has ten coins." But then our evidence for p does have a bearing on q—indeed, is capable of justifying q. Granted too, since Jones is not in fact the man who will get the job, q is not in fact about Jones. But since a belief can be justified without being true, what a belief is in fact about has no bearing on whether it is justified. Since we are justified in believing *p,* we are also justified in believing that *q* is about Jones, and this is enough to underwrite transferring our justification to *q.*

Thus, the principle of implicit justification is able to withstand criticism, and it can be legitimately used to justify absolute truth claims.

3. THE IMPORTANCE OF ABSOLUTE TRUTH

James find the concept of absolute truth arid and useless. He thinks that the interesting question is whether the given proposition has any claim on us to be believed.[8] In one way, he is right. We cannot decide whether something is absolutely true without deciding whether it does have a claim on our beliefs, and once we have decided the latter question, there is nothing more we can, or need, do. Considerations of absolute truth can therefore seem to be an inconsequential appendix to the body of human inquiry.

Although truth claims are derivative, this is not a reason to abandon the concept of truth. There is still a point in saying "That is true" as well as "That is justified" or "That is certain." For one thing, we *are* justified in making the truth claim and this should not be ignored, at least for theoretical purposes. Moreover, and more significantly, the whole point of investigating whether given beliefs are justified is to arrive at a position where we can justifiably say that things actually are as we believe them to be. In short, an ideal investigation just *is* the search for absolute truth. Dispensing with the concept of truth would be like abandoning the concept of wealth upon finding out that achieving a certain income level is both necessary and sufficient for being wealthy. Talk about wealth might then make no difference in practice. But it would still play a role in formulating our economic aspirations. Similarly, we need the concept of truth in order to state our intellectual aspirations. Finally, we should retain the concept in order to formulate, and thereby leave open, the question of whether an access to absolute truth is secured by, or restricted to, our becoming justifiably sure of things.

4. OBSERVATIONAL ACCESS

Some might think that our observations are too theory-laden to give us access to absolute truth. For example, Popper says that "every statement has the character of a theory" and Hanson that "observaton of x is shaped by prior knowledge of x."[9] Now, observations do generally go beyond what we immediately perceive and they are shaped by what we antecedently believe. Hence they cannot provide good independent evidence for *those* beliefs. For example, if Tycho observes the sun's rising partly because he believes that the sun revolves around the earth, his observation cannot advance the case for his theoretical belief. But observations are not parasitical on every belief. Someone can observe a glass of water in front of him without doing so just because he expects the glass to be there. His observation can then provide good support for believing that a glass exists. Granted, the observation might well draw on other considerations, such as the philosophical hypothesis that external objects exist. In that case the observation cannot be used to support the external-world hypothesis. But it can still help provide strong support for believing that the glass exists, given that the external-world hypothesis can be independently defended. Thus, theory-ladenness does not block our access to truth.

5. COMPREHENSIVE TRUTH

Some who concede that we can justifiably claim the truth of what we purportedly know might still not concede that we can do the same for the comprehensive truth requirement. They might feel that unless we possess the absolutely total evidence, we cannot claim that there is *no* truth such that our knowing it would have destroyed our justification for being sure. And as finite beings we cannot possess the absolutely total evidence.[10]

We have already seen that we can justifiably believe that no good counterevidence will ever turn up, provided we have reliable evidence (see chapter 9, section 2). We do not have to possess the absolutely total evidence in order to achieve this much. But this means that we can justifiably believe that, for any proposition the knowledge of which would have destroyed our justification for being sure, there is conclusive evidence against the proposition. Hence we can justifiably believe of any such proposition that it is false. Thus, we can justifiably believe that the comprehensive truth requirement is satisfied without having to possess the absolutely total evidence. We not only have access to the truth of what we know, we also have access to the remaining truths that are required by our knowing.

6. SUMMARY

Although knowledge involves truth, and truth is absolute, this does not create a basis for scepticism. Claiming truth does not embrace a suspect metaphysics. And being justifiably sure of things is enough to justify our claiming that the comprehensive truth requirement is satisfied. Moreover, although the justification of truth claims is a derivative affair, we should retain the concept of absolute truth, both to formulate our intellectual aspirations and to keep open the question of whether we really do have access to absolute truth via justified belief.

CHAPTER FOURTEEN
Conclusion

1. FURTHER SCEPTICAL ARGUMENTS

My intention has not been to consider every possible philosophical reason for disclaiming knowledge. Indeed, there is no way in which one could ever tell when such a feat had been accomplished. My aim has simply been to consider a representative sample. Of course, other arguments can be found in the literature. For example, Unger argues that we are rarely, if ever, absolutely sure of anything, on the ground that absolutes rarely exist in nature.[1] His premise is unconvincing, since, e.g., natural containers are often entirely empty of things of a specified sort, which is analogous to our judging that there is absolutely no good counterevidence with respect to a given proposition. But replying to this and other arguments is not the important thing to do right now. The important consideration is whether the replies given to date constitute a reliable body of evidence—i.e., whether we can on their basis say that there probably are effective answers for additional arguments, even though we do not have such answers—indeed, even though we cannot foresee what all the arguments will be like. My judgment—and it *is* a judgment—is that they do.

2. THE INDISPENSABILITY OF PHILOSOPHY

No one is in a position to make such a judgment unless he has actually done some philosophy. Philosophical doubts are sufficiently distinctive that someone with a good track record in coping with ordinary grounds for doubt still lacks the meta evidence to say that a given philosophical objection is probably unsound. He first has to work out some answers for himself (unless he can appeal to philosophical authority, which seems a doubtful move). This is why many novices are so perplexed when they first confront scepticism. Their basic assumptions are challenged in an unprecedented way, and until they can actually meet this type of challenge in a variety of instances, they can do nothing except dismiss the sceptic dogmatically.[2]

This means that no one knows anything unless he has done philosophy. At first this might seem an odd result. It implies that the uninitiated fail to know that they exist or that $2 + 2 = 4$. But we must remember just how demanding the concept of knowledge is in this context. It requires a knower to be justified in holding that there is absolutely no good counterevidence, judged by the highest standards. This requires a warrant for saying that there is no good philosophical reason for doubt, and such a warrant is not easily purchased. When knowledge is conceived as a prized possession, we should not be surprised if it turns out to be hard to come by.

The important thing to realize, of course, is that the task is not hopeless, that philosophy can meet sceptical challenges in a way that underwrites optimism. Socratic wisdom at one level consists in a recognition of our own ignorance. But at another level it involves a recognition that philosophy can manage to transform ignorance into knowledge. Granted, Socrates describes the transition in a way that tends to put it beyond the reach of embodied human beings. But there is a significantly ideal concept of knowledge that manages to avoid such a fate.

3. LEAVING THE QUESTION OPEN

We do have knowledge in those situations where we normally and responsibly think that we do. A claim that we satisfy the conditions of knowing can be defended in a way that indicates that it will probably be just as defensible in the face of new considerations. Granted, this is a fallible judgment, both as an account of the present strength of our evidence and as a prediction of what is apt to happen in the future. A sceptic can challenge the account by arguing, e.g., that I have underestimated one of his arguments, or that the range of arguments in the sample is too narrow given the varied support available for other-minds scepticism, for scepticism about translation, for scepticism about reidentifiable particulars, and for scepticism about the past. Or he can falsify the prediction by offering an actual argument that resists a satisfactory answer. There is a possibility that such challenges will succeed. But as long as successful challenges are no more than possible, we can rightfully claim knowledge in an ideal sense. We can be justifiably sure of things, even though we cannot be sure that those things are certain and even though our justification may eventually disappear.

Notes

CHAPTER 1

1. For nonminimal concepts of plausibility, see G. Polya, *Patterns of Plausible Inference*, vols. 1 and 2 (Princeton, Princeton University Press, 1954, 1969); N. Rescher, *The Coherence Theory of Truth* (Oxford, Clarendon Press, 1973).

2. See John Locke, *An Essay Concerning Human Understanding*, bk. 4, chs. 2, 7.

3. See, respectively, K. Lehrer, *Knowledge* (Oxford, Clarendon Press, 1974), p. 102; M. Williams, *Groundless Belief* (New Haven, Yale University Press, 1977), p. 84; and D. Armstrong, *Belief, Truth and Knowledge* (Cambridge, Cambridge University Press, 1971), p. 157.

4. B. Russell, *Human Knowledge: Its Scope and Limits* (London, Allen and Unwin, 1948), p. 411.

5. H. H. Price, *Perception* (London, Methuen, 1932), pp. 185–186.

6. M. Williams, *Groundless Belief*, p. 111.

7. G. Harman, *Thought* (Princeton, Princeton University Press, 1973), p. 12.

8. Contrast Lehrer, *Knowledge*, p. 102.

CHAPTER 2

1. See K. Popper, "On Rules of Detachment and So-called Deductive Logic", in I. Lakatos (ed.), *Inductive Logic* (Amsterdam, North-Holland, 1968), pp. 137–38.

2. J. M. Keynes, *A Treatise on Probability* (London, Macmillan, 1921); R. Carnap, *The Logical Foundations of Probability* (Chicago, University of Chicago Press, 1950).

3. See A. J. Ayer, "The Concept of Probability as a Logical Relation," *The Concept of a Person* (London, Macmillan, 1963).

4. For surveys of standard theories, see W. Salmon, *The Foundations of Scientific Inference* (Pittsburgh, Pittsburgh University Press, 1966); A. Michalos, *Principles of Logic* (Englewood Cliffs, Prentice-Hall, 1969); B. Skyrms, *Choice and Chance* (Belmont, Wadsworth, 1966); J. L. Mackie, *Truth, Probability, and Paradox* (Oxford, Clarendon Press, 1973).

5. Compare W. Kneale, *Probability and Induction* (Oxford, Clarendon Press, 1949), p. 173.

6. Contrast W. Salmon, *The Foundations of Scientific Inference*, p. 66.

7. Keynes, *A Treatise on Probability*, ch. 4.

8. Compare Popper, *The Logic of Scientific Discovery* (London, Hutchinson, 1959), pp. 407–8.

9. For discussion, see I. Levi, *Gambling with Truth* (New York, Knopf, 1967); Lakatos (ed.), *Inductive Logic;* M. Swain (ed.), *Induction, Acceptance and Rational Belief* (Dordrecht, Reidel, 1970).

10. See Lehrer, "Reason and Consistency," in Lehrer (ed.), *Analysis and Metaphysics* (Dordrecht, Reidel, 1975), pp. 57–74.

11. Compare Kyburg, "Conjunctivitis," in Swain (ed.), *Induction, Acceptance and Rational Belief*, pp. 55–82.

CHAPTER 3

1. R. Firth, "The Anatomy of Certainty," *Philosophical Review* 76 (1967): 3–27.

2. A. Quinton, *The Nature of Things* (London, Routledge and Kegan Paul, 1973), p. 148.

3. Compare Popper, *Objective Knowledge* (Oxford, Clarendon Press, 1972), p. 78; E. Wolgast, *Paradoxes of Knowledge* (Ithaca, Cornell University Press, 1977), p. 54; Annis, "A Contextualist Theory of Epistemic Justification," *American Philosophical Quarterly* 15 (1978):213–19.

4. C. S. Peirce, *Collected Papers,* ed. C. Hartshorne and P. Weiss (Cambridge, Harvard University Press, 1934), vol. 5.

5. Compare B. Williams, *Descartes* (Harmondsworth, Penguin, 1978), ch. 2.

CHAPTER 4

1. P. F. Strawson, "A Problem About Truth—a Reply to Mr. Warnock," in G. Pitcher (ed.), *Truth* (Englewood Cliffs, Prentice-Hall, 1964), pp. 68–84; compare F. P. Ramsey, *Foundations of Mathematics* (London, Routledge and Kegan Paul, 1931), p. 142.

2. A. Prior, *Objects of Thought* (Oxford, Clarendon Press, 1971), chs. 1–3; C. J. F. Williams, *What Is Truth?* (Cambridge, Cambridge University Press, 1976), chs. 1–2.

3. D. L. Grover, J. L. Camp, and N. D. Belnap, Jr., "A Prosentential Theory of Truth," *Philosophical Studies* 27 (1975):73–125.

4. See Bas C. Van Fraassen, "Presupposition, Implication, and Self-reference," *Journal of Philosophy* 65 (1968):136–52; "Truth and Paradoxical Consequences," R. L. Martin (ed.), *The Paradox of the Liar* (New Haven, Yale University Press, 1970).

5. Grover, "Inheritors and Paradox," *Journal of Philosophy* 74 (1977): 590–604.

6. See T. Burge, "Semantical Paradox," *Journal of Philosophy* 76 (1979):169–98, and his references.

7. Contrast W. V. O. Quine, *Philosophy of Logic* (Englewood Cliffs, Prentice-Hall, 1970), p. 45; "The Ways of Paradox," *The Ways of Paradox and Other Essays* (New York, Random House, 1966).

8. See H. Herzberger, "Paradoxes of Grounding in Semantics," *Journal of Philosophy* 67 (1970):145–67.

9. B. Russell, "Philosophy of Logical Atomism," *Logic and Knowledge* (London, Allen and Unwin, 1956), p. 183.

10. D. Hamlyn, *Theory of Knowledge* (New York, Doubleday, 1970), pp. 138–39.

11. Mackie, *Truth, Probability, and Paradox,* p. 55.

12. R. Chisholm, *Theory of Knowledge,* (Englewood Cliffs, Prentice-Hall, 1966), ch. 7; 2d ed., ch. 5.

13. Compare J. Williamson, "Facts and Truth," *Philosophical Quarterly* 26 (1976):203–16.

CHAPTER 5

1. The example is from N. Champawat and J. T. Saunders, "Mr. Clark's Definition of 'Knowledge,'" *Analysis* 25 (1964–65):8–9.

2. Contrast D. Annis, "Knowledge, Belief, and Rationality," *Journal of Philosophy* 74 (1977):217–25, and his references.

3. Z. Vendler, *Res Cogitans* (Ithaca, Cornell University Press, 1972), ch. 5. For criticism, see O. R. Jones, "Can One Believe What One Knows?" *Philosophical Review* 84 (1975):220–35.

4. See Hamlyn, *Theory of Knowledge,* pp. 84–85.

5. Lehrer, *Knowledge,* ch. 3.

6. N. Malcolm, "Knowledge and Belief," *Knowledge and Certainty* (Englewood Cliffs, Prentice-Hall, 1963); L. J. Cohen, "More About Knowing and Being Sure," *Analysis* 27 (1966–67):11–16. Malcolm adopts a less rigid view on pp. 288–89, *Knowledge and Certainty.*

7. Ayer, *Problem of Knowledge* (London, Macmillan, 1956), p. 16. He adopts a more moderate view in *Metaphysics and Common Sense* (San Francisco, Freeman Cooper, 1970), p. 117.

8. Ayer, *Problem of Knowledge,* pp. 33–34.

9. Alvin Goldman, "Discrimination and Perceptual Knowledge," *Journal of Philosophy* 73 (1976):771–91.

10. K. Lehrer and T. Paxson, Jr., "Knowledge: Undefeated Justified True Belief," *Journal of Philosophy* 66 (1969):225–37.

11. Harman, *Thought,* p. 143.

12. R. Almeder, "Defeasibility and Scepticism," *Australasian Journal of Philosophy* 51 (1973):238–44.

13. Harman, *Thought,* p. 152.

14. E. Sosa, "Propositional Knowledge," *Philosophical Studies* 20 (1969):33–43.

15. Sosa, Review of Lehrer: *Knowledge, Journal of Philosophy* 73 (1976):812–21.

16. M. Clark, Review of Lehrer: *Knowledge, Mind* 86 (1977):142–44.

17. D. Locke, review of C. Ginet: *Knowledge, Perception, and Memory, Philosophical Quarterly* 26 (1976):279–80.

18. Sosa, "Two Conceptions of Knowledge," *Journal of Philosophy* 67 (1970):59–66.

19. Compare Chisholm, "On the Nature of Empirical Evidence," in Chisholm and R. Swartz (eds.), *Empirical Knowledge* (Englewood Cliffs, Prentice-Hall, 1973), pp. 237–39.

CHAPTER 6

1. G. E. Moore, "Defence of Common Sense," *Philosophical Papers* (London, Allen and Unwin, 1959), p. 43.

2. Moore, "Proof of an External World," *Philosophical Papers,* p. 146.

3. Moore, *Some Main Problems of Philosophy* (London, Allen and Unwin, 1953), pp. 119–20.

4. Malcolm, "George Edward Moore," *Knowledge and Certainty,* p. 181.

5. L. Wittgenstein, *On Certainty* (Oxford, Blackwell, 1969), sec. 456.

6. Wittgenstein, *On Certainty,* sec. 115.

7. H. Prichard, *Knowledge and Perception* (Oxford, Clarendon Press, 1950), p. 86.

8. For further discussion, see Cornman, "On Acceptability Without Certainty," *Journal of Philosophy* 74 (1977):29–47.

CHAPTER 7

1. Compare Ayer, *Problem of Knowledge,* p. 52.

2. Compare Wittgenstein, *Philosophical Investigations* (Oxford, Blackwell,

1953), secs. 246, 408; F. L. Will, *Induction and Justification* (Ithaca, Cornell University Press, 1974), pt. 2.

3. Malcolm, "Knowledge and Belief," p. 63.

4. C. Hempel, "On the Nature of Mathematical Truth," *American Mathematical Monthly* 52 (1945):543–56. Contrast Quine, "Two Dogmas of Empiricism," *From a Logical Point of View* (Cambridge, Harvard University Press, 1953), pp. 20–46.

5. Compare H. Putnam, *Mathematics, Matter, and Method, Philosophical Papers*, vol. 1 (Cambridge, Cambridge University Press, 1975); H. Lehman, *Introduction to the Philosophy of Mathematics* (Oxford, Blackwell, 1979), ch. 8.

6. Contrast Quine, "Necessary Truth," *The Ways of Paradox*, p. 56.

7. H. P. Grice and P. F. Strawson, "In Defense of a Dogma," *Philosophical Review* 65 (1956):141–58.

8. E. Nagel, "Logic Without Ontology," in Y. Krikorian (ed.), *Naturalism and the Human Spirit* (New York, Columbia University Press, 1944).

9. J. Pollock, *Knowledge and Justification*, (Princeton, Princeton University Press), p. 76. He concedes that the reports he finds incorrigible are "extremely weak" and that "by themselves they do not get us very far" (pp. 78–79).

10. Malcolm, "Direct Perception," *Knowledge and Certainty*, pp. 73–95.

11. Wittgenstein, *On Certainty*, sec. 498. Also, Malcolm, *Thought and Knowledge* (Ithaca, Cornell University Press, 1977), p. 196; Wolgast, *Paradoxes of Knowledge*, p. 194.

12. Wittgenstein, *On Certainty*, sec. 613.

13. Wittgenstein, *On Certainty*, sec. 614.

14. Wittgenstein, *On Certainty*, sec. 92.

15. Wittgenstein, *On Certainty*, sec. 245.

16. Wittgenstein, *On Certainty*, sec. 516.

CHAPTER 8

1. Contrast Lehrer, "Why Not Scepticism?" *Philosophical Forum* 2 (1971):283–98.

2. Compare Popper, *Objective Knowledge*, p. 79.

3. Malcolm, "The Verification Argument," *Knowledge and Certainty*, pp. 38–40.

4. Some fallibilists seek to avoid scepticism; e.g., J. H. Newman, *Grammar of Assent*, ch. 2, sec. 2; J. L. Austin, "Other Minds," *Proceedings of the Aristotelian Society, Supplementary Volume* 20 (1946):148–87; A. J. Ayer, *Problem of Knowledge*, pp. 44, 66–68; D. Hamlyn, *Theory of Knowledge*, p. 254; N. Rescher, *The Coherence Theory of Truth*, ch. 13.

5. W. James, "The Will to Believe," in A. Castell (ed.), *Essays in Pragmatism* (New York, Hafner, 1948), pp. 95–99.

6. Peirce, "Lessons from the History of Science," *Collected Papers*, vol. 1.

7. See W. Rozeboom, "Why I Know So Much More Than You Do," *American Philosophical Quarterly* 4 (1967):281–90.

8. R. Hilpinen, "Knowing That One Knows and the Classical Definition of Knowledge," *Synthese* 21 (1970):109–32.

9. J. Hintikka, "'Knowing That One Knows' Reviewed," *Synthese* 21 (1970):141–62.

10. See Harman, "Induction," in Swain (ed.), *Induction, Acceptance, and Rational Belief*, pp. 83–99.

11. Harman, *Thought*, p. 148.

12. I. Hacking, "Possibility," *Philosophical Review* 76 (1967), p. 168.

13. Lehrer, *Knowledge*, p. 239.

14. Popper, *Objective Knowledge*, p. 80.

15. Lakatos, *Proofs and Refutations* (Cambridge University Press, 1976), pp. 4, 27, 37, 41.

16. Unger, *Ignorance*, pp. 107–17.

17. Malcolm, "The Verification Argument," *Knowledge and Certainty*, pp. 1–57.

18. Contrast R. Suter, "The Dream Argument," *American Philosophical Quarterly* 13 (1976):185–94.

19. Moore, "Certainty," *Philosophical Papers*, pp. 227–51.

20. Malcolm, *Dreaming* (London, Routledge and Kegan Paul, 1959), pp. 51–57.

21. Contrast E. M. Curley, *Descartes Against the Sceptics* (Cambridge, Harvard University Press, 1978), ch. 3.

CHAPTER 9

1. Lehrer, *Knowledge*, p. 198.

2. For another belief-oriented account, see Pollock, *Knowledge and Justification*, pp. 39–46.

3. D. Hume, *A Treatise of Human Nature*, bk. I, ch. iii, sec. 12.

4. Popper, *Objective Knowledge*, pp. 10–11, 97.

5. P. Duhem, *The Aim and Structure of Physical Theory* (Princeton, Princeton University Press, 1954), p. 190.

6. Compare Salmon, Barker, and Kyburg, "Symposium on Inductive Inference," *American Philosophical Quarterly* 2 (1965):265–80.

7. Russell, *Problems of Philosophy* (London, Oxford University Press, 1912), ch. 6.

8. Strawson, *Introduction to Logical Theory* (London, Methuen, 1952), p. 257.

9. Barker, "Is There a Problem of Induction?" *American Philosophical Quarterly* 2 (1965): 272.

10. Salmon, "Inductive Inference," B. Baumrin (ed.), *Philosophy of Science: The Delaware Seminar*, vol. 2 (New York, Wiley, 1963), pp. 353–70.

11. M. Black, "Self-supporting Inductive Arguments," *Journal of Philosophy* 55 (1958):718–25.

12. See S. Haack, "The Justification of Deduction," *Mind* 85 (1976):112–19.

CHAPTER 10

1. Hempel, "Studies in the Logic of Confirmation," *Mind* 54 (1945):1–26, 97–121.

2. Compare Hempel, "Studies in the Logic of Confirmation"; Mackie, "The Paradox of Confirmation," *British Journal for the Philosophy of Science* 13 (1963):265–77; I. Scheffler, *The Anatomy of Inquiry* (New York, Knopf, 1963); L. J. Cohen, *The Implications of Induction* (London, Methuen, 1970), ch. 3.

3. N. Goodman, *Fact, Fiction, and Forecast* (London, University of London Press, 1955), ch. 3.

4. See Carnap, *The Logical Foundations of Probability*, pt. 6; Skyrms, "Nomological Necessity and the Paradoxes of Confirmation," *Philosophy of Science* 34 (1966):230–49.

5. B. Brody, "Confirmation and Explanation," *Journal of Philosophy* 65 (1968):282–99.

6. J. W. N. Watkins, "Confirmation, the Paradoxes, and Positivism," M. Bunge (ed.), *The Critical Approach to Science and Philosophy* (New York, Free Press, 1964).

7. Goodman, *Fact, Fiction, and Forecast*, chs. 3, 4.

8. Contrast Achinstein-Barker, "On the New Riddle of Induction," *Philosophical Review* 69 (1960):511–22.

9. The example is from S. Blackburn, *Reason and Prediction* (Cambridge, Cambridge University Press, 1973), pp. 64–65.

10. Blackburn, *Reason and Prediction*, p. 73.

11. See F. Jackson, "Grue," *Journal of Philosophy* 72 (1975):113–31.

12. Skyrms, *Choice and Chance*, pp. 61–62.

CHAPTER 11

1. A fourth challenge would be to adopt a causal-type analysis that eliminates a need for foundations. But this would not help the noncausal analysis of knowledge offered in chapter 5. See Armstrong, *Belief, Truth and Knowledge*, chs. 11–13.

2. See Ayer, "Knowledge, Belief and Evidence," *Metaphysics and Common Sense*, pp. 64–81.

3. See Peirce, "Questions Concerning Certain Faculties Claimed for Man," question 7, *Collected Papers*, vol. 5; R. Foley, "Inferential Justification and the Infinite Regress," *American Philosophical Quarterly* 15 (1978):311–16.

4. Lehrer, *Knowledge*, p. 198.

5. Rescher, "Foundationalism, Coherentism, and the Idea of Cognitive Systematization," *Journal of Philosophy* 71 (1974): 699.

6. Rescher, *Coherence Theory of Truth*, p. 56.

7. L. Bonjour, "The Coherence Theory of Empirical Knowledge," *Philosophical Studies* 30 (1976): 281–312.

8. Compare accounts of weak foundationalism in Lehrer, *Knowledge*, ch. 5; Quinton, *The Nature of Things*, pt. 2; Pastin, "Modest Foundationalism and Self-warrant"; Annis, "Epistemic Foundationalism"; Alston, "Has Foundationalism Been Refuted?" *Philosophical Studies* 29 (1976):287–305.

9. Contrast Quinton, *The Nature of Things;* Alston, "Two Types of Foundationalism," *Journal of Philosophy* 73 (1976):165–85; Cornman, "Foundational versus Nonfoundational Theories of Empirical Justification."

10. Goodman, *The Structure of Appearance* (Cambridge, Harvard University Press, 1951), p. 104.

11. I. T. Oakley, "An Argument for Scepticism Concerning Justified Beliefs," *American Philosophical Quarterly* 13 (1976):221–28.

12. Bonjour, "Can Empirical Knowledge Have a Foundation?" *American Philosophical Quarterly* 15 (1978):1–14.

13. Contrast Price, *Belief* (London, Allen and Unwin, 1969), p. 106.

14. Malcolm, *Knowledge and Certainty*, p. 230. Also see R. Squires, "Memory Unchained," *Philosophical Review* 77 (1969):178–97. For criticism, see Pollock, *Knowledge and Justfication*, pp. 190–95.

CHAPTER 12

1. G. Berkeley, *Three Dialogues Between Hylas and Philonous*, First Dialogue.

2. Price, *Perception*, p. 3.

3. Malcolm, "Direct Perception," *Knowledge and Certainty*.

4. Jackson, *Perception* (Cambridge, Cambridge University Press, 1977), pp. 9–10.

5. Austin, *Sense and Sensibilia* (Oxford, Clarendon Press, 1962), p. 116.

6. For example, Locke, *An Essay Concerning Human Understanding*, bk. IV, ch. xi; Russell, *Problems of Philosophy*, ch. 1.

7. See Russell, *Problems of Philosophy;* Mackie, *Problems from Locke* (Oxford, Clarendon Press, 1976), ch. 2; Jackson, *Perception.*

8. S. Kripke, "Identity and Necessity," M. K. Munitz (ed.), *Identity and Individuation* (New York, 1971), pp. 135–64.

9. Contrast R. Chisholm, *Perceiving* (Ithaca, Cornell University Press, 1957), p. 115; F. Dretske, *Seeing and Knowing* (London, Routledge and Kegan Paul, 1969), p. 65; G. Pitcher, *A Theory of Perception* (Princeton University Press, 1971) pp. 32–38.

10. Austin, *Sense and Sensibilia,* pp. 44–45.

11. Contrast W. H. F. Barnes, "The Myth of Sense-Data," *Proceedings Aristotelian Society* 45 (1944–45); Armstrong, *Perception and the Physical World* (London, Routledge and Kegan Paul, 1961), pp. 220–21.

12. Barnes, "The Myth of Sense-Data."

13. Compare Ayer, *Problem of Knowledge,* pp. 109–11.

14. Compare W. James, *Principles of Psychology* (New York, Holt, 1890), vol. 1, ch. 16; Broad, *Scientific Thought* (London, Routledge and Kegan Paul, 1923), ch. 10.

15. Austin, *Sense and Sensibilia,* pp. 87–103.

16. Locke, *An Essay Concerning Human Understanding,* bk. IV, ch. xi.

17. Berkeley, *Principles Concerning Human Knowledge,* sec. 8.

CHAPTER 13

1. Unger, *Ignorance,* ch. 7.

2. Peirce, "Illustrations of the Logic of Science," *Collected Papers,* vol. 5.

3. Lehrer, *Knowledge,* p. 48.

4. Lehrer, *Knowledge,* p. 227.

5. Wolgast, *Paradoxes of Knowledge,* ch. 1.

6. R. Richman, "Justified True Belief as Knowledge," *Canadian Journal of Philosophy* 4 (1975): 435–39.

7. I. Thalberg, "In Defense of Justified True Belief," *Journal of Philosophy* 66 (1969):794–803. Also see J. Margolis, "The Problem of Justified Belief," *Philosophical Studies* 23 (1972):405–9; C. Pailthorp, "Knowledge as Justified True Belief," *Review of Metaphysics* 23 (1969):25–47.

8. James, "Pragmatism's Conception of Truth," *Essays in Pragmatism.*

9. Popper, *Logic of Scientific Discovery,* pp. 94–95; N. R. Hanson, *Patterns of Discovery* (Cambridge, Cambridge University Press, 1958), p. 19.

10. See S. R. Levy, "Defeasibility Theories of Knowledge," *Canadian Journal of Philosophy* 7 (1977):115–24.

CHAPTER 14

1. Unger, *Ignorance,* p. 49. For further criticism, see J. Cargile, "In Reply to A Defense of Skepticism,'" *Philosophical Review* 81 (1972):229–36; O. A. Johnson, *Skepticism and Cognitivism* (Los Angeles, University of California Press, 1978), ch. 5.

2. Compare Unger, *Ignorance,* pp. 3–4.

Name Index

Only authors referred to in the body of the text are indexed.

Almeder, R., 67
Armstrong, D., 13
Austin, J. L., 58, 139, 144, 147
Ayer, A. J., 147

Barker, S., 111
Belnap, N., 43
Berkeley, G., 137, 150
Black, M., 112
Bonjour, L., 127, 132
Brody, B., 116

Camp, J., 43
Carnap, R., 22
Chisholm, R., 52
Clark, M., 70

Descartes, R., 75
Duhem, P., 108, 109

Firth, R., 36, 37

Goodman, N., 109, 116, 118, 119, 131
Grice, H. P., 83
Grover, D., 43, 44

Hacking, I., 95
Hamlyn, D. W., 52
Hanson, N., 156
Harman, G., 15, 66, 68, 94
Hempel, C., 82, 115
Hilpinen, R., 92
Hintikka, J., 93

Jackson, F., 119, 120, 141
James, W., 90, 91, 156

Keynes, J. M., 22, 27
Kripke, S., 142

Lakatos, I., 96
Lehrer, K., 13, 16, 60, 65, 95, 105, 126, 154

Locke, D., 70
Locke, J., 12, 148

Mackie, J. L., 52
Malcolm, N., 60, 76, 82, 85, 89, 97, 99, 100, 135
Moore, G. E., 75, 76, 99

Nagel, E., 84

Oakley, I., 131

Paxson, T., 65
Peirce, C. S., 39, 91, 92, 154
Pollock, J., 84
Popper, K., 95, 156
Price, H. H., 15
Prichard, H. A., 77

Quinton, A., 37
Reichenbach, H., 111
Rescher, N., 126
Richman, R., 155
Russell, B., 15, 49, 50, 52, 110

Salmon, W., 111
Skyrms, B., 121
Socrates, 160
Sosa, E., 68, 69, 71
Strawson, P. F., 42, 83, 110, 111

Thalberg, I., 155

Unger, P., 96, 97, 152, 153, 159

Vendler, Z., 59

Watkins, J., 117
Williams, M., 13, 15
Wittgenstein, L., 77, 85–87
Wolgast, E., 154

Subject Index

Absolutes, 23–26, 32–33, 40–41
Analyticity, 82–84

Belief, 31–32, 56–61

Certainty, 13–14, 31–39, 61–62, 88–101
Coherence theory, 125–27
Confirmation, 114–22
Correspondence theory, 52–54, 153

Deduction, 112–13
Degeneracy, 47–48
Dogmatism, 79–87, 93–97

Entities, 10–11, 52–54, 141–48, 152–53
Evidence, 7–8, 15, 19–20, 23, 148–50

Fallibilism, 90–93
Foundationalism, 123–35

Guaranteed propositions, 80–81

Immediacy, 127–29, 136–39
Inconsistency, 28–30
Incorrigibility, 34, 84–85, 134
Indifference, 26–28
Indubitability, 37–38
Induction, 106–12
Intuition, 11–14, 63, 127–29

Justification, 36–37, 62–67, 102–13, 123–35, 153–56

Knowledge, 23, 30, 56–72

Necessity, 34–36, 61–62, 82–84

Objectivity, 10, 22, 41
Objects, 138–39, 150

Paradox, 44–52, 114–22
Perception, 136–51
Phenomena, 141–50
Plausibility, 5–17
Practice, 32–39
Probability, 6, 18–30
Projection, 118–22
Prosentential theory, 43–44

Reality, 10, 42–44
Redundancy theory, 42–43
Reference, 45–48
Representationalism, 140–41, 143–44

Scepticism, 1, 36, 56, 75–80, 88–101, 123, 127, 159–61
Subjectivity, 9–10, 22, 105–6, 133–35
Sureness, 31–32, 56–58

Testability, 97–98, 117–18
Toleration, 79–87, 160–61
Truth, 10, 12, 18, 33–34, 40–55, 67–72, 152–58